Simon King's
NATURE WATCH

HOW TO TRACK AND OBSERVE WILDLIFE

quadrille

In fondest memory of my friend and mentor,
Mike Kendall. He was my key-master.

Publishing Director: Sarah Lavelle
Creative Director: Helen Lewis
Editor: Jinny Johnson
Design: Smith & Gilmour
Production: Tom Moore, Vincent Smith

First published in 2016 by
Quadrille Publishing
Pentagon House
52–54 Southwark Street
London SE1 1UN
www.quadrille.co.uk

Quadrille is an imprint of Hardie Grant
www.hardiegrant.com.au

Text © Simon King 2016
Photography © Simon King 2016
Design and layout © Quadrille Publishing 2016

Cataloguing in Publication Data: a catalogue record for
this book is available from the British Library.

ISBN: 978 184949 4762

Printed in China

PICTURE CREDITS
Photographs: all photos by Simon King except for the following:
Phil Mumby: 189, 195, 206, 212, 230 (top left), 235 (top right)
Charlie Nash: 20
Charlie Phillips: 174
Marguerite Smits van Oyen: 12, 25
Sam Stewart: 46, 122, 217, 221, 224
Chris Terry: front cover, 255
Alex Tivenan: 8, 10, 15, 16, 23

Animal illustrations: Jake Davis
Footprint illustrations: Simon King

CONTENTS

INTRODUCTION

From the earliest age I have had a passionate interest in wildlife. My desire to know more about my natural neighbours drew me to the bottom of the garden looking for insects and toads, and, when I was old enough, to the woods and rivers around my childhood home in southwest England to watch kingfishers, sparrowhawks, foxes and more.

Since then, in my work as a naturalist and wildlife film-maker, I have encountered a phenomenal variety of creatures, from the big cats of Kenya to the killer whales of Patagonia. But it is in my home-patch of the UK that I have invested the greatest time and focus on learning the ways of the wild.

Over the past five decades I have tried to develop methods to help me close the gap between myself and other creatures. I have strived to learn their language, to read the clues they leave behind and to remain undetected so that I can observe them without affecting their behaviour.

This book is a distillation of some of that knowledge. It is not an identification guide to the wildlife of Britain and Europe, although many of the pictures of the animals described should help the reader identify them in the field.

Instead the book is designed to be a key – a key to the door of your wild neighbours. With its help, you should be able to tell who has been visiting, and digging up, your garden, and which animal left the track – or the poo – on the path. You will learn how to move, look and listen, even how to smell what's around you, with fresh, heightened senses. And in so doing, the door to the wild world will slowly swing open and you will find yourself surrounded by wonder, beauty, drama and pathos.

If a species has been included, it is because I believe that it leaves signs that may help with identifying its whereabouts, and/or there are techniques you can deploy that may help you observe the animal in the wild. Limitations of space, as well as my desire to describe only species of which I have first-hand knowledge, mean that some animals that may warrant inclusion have been omitted, and for this I apologise. I am always learning and aiming to fill the gaps.

Sense graphics

For many species, I have rated their senses on a scale of 1–10. I have only included this information for animals that have the potential to be adversely affected by the presence of a human, and frequently use their senses to smell, hear or see a human. With this in mind, the number rating reflects the importance of each sense when considering how you should go about watching that animal.

Rabbits, for instance, have a keen sense of smell and can tell each other apart by scent alone. But they are unlikely to be bothered by the smell of a human sitting upwind of them, so this sense rates only a 3 on their scale. If a rabbit hears or sees a human, it is likely to run for cover; so the rabbit's senses of hearing and sight, both of which are keen, are given a rating of 8.

Finally, may I implore you to show the greatest respect to the creatures you are trying to observe. With time, patience and care you will be able to enter their world without causing a ripple and that is a truly beautiful experience. I wish you good luck, good light and a favourable wind.

Peace and light, Simon King

EQUIPMENT

OPTICS

BINOCULARS

If there is one essential tool for the field naturalist it is a pair of binoculars. They all aim to do a similar job (bring objects you are looking at into close detail), but they have vastly different specifications and levels of quality.

The first thing to bear in mind is that bigger is not better. The claim for a pair of binoculars might be that they magnify an object by 20 or 30 times, but that does not make them the best pair to purchase.

There are three main types of binoculars: Porro prism and roof prism in the full-size models, and a range of compact models.

As the name suggests, the Porro and roof designs are distinguished by their configuration of internal prisms. The roof prism has a straight barrel design, with the exit pupil (the lens nearest the eye) in line with the object lens (the big lens furthest from the eye). Porro prism binoculars have the offset form of the 'typical' binocular in which the object lens is set wider than the exit pupil.

All top-of-the-range sports optics binoculars have the roof prism as their leading design. Indeed, most naturalists now choose roof prism over Porro prism, citing comfort and ease of use as driving factors in their choice. Both types work equally well and much of the decision on what style you go for comes down to personal choice based on 'feel' and, of course, price.

Compact binoculars are designed for occasional use when you might not be able to carry a full-size pair of binoculars. They generally suffer from low light transmission due to their small object lenses.

Specification

When choosing a pair of binoculars for watching wildlife, the following are the key features to look out for.

Magnification

I find the ideal magnification for wildlife watching to be between 7x and 10x. Any less and you will struggle to pick out the detail necessary for bird identification or well-camouflaged mammals; any more and you will find it hard to hand-hold your binoculars steady enough for a clear view.

Generally speaking, the lower the magnification, the brighter and wider the image. There are exceptions with a few top-of-the-range optics, which manage to achieve astonishing brightness and field of view while maintaining higher magnifications.

Contrast and colour

When testing optics, try comparing inexpensive models with the most expensive. While they may appear superficially similar, you will notice key differences in the image, and much of this comes down to the quality of the optics housed in the unit. Optical glass is coated to address the problems created by refraction of light, specifically the colour spectrum. Poor optics will reveal colour 'fringing', where the image appears to have rainbow edges on all but the very centre of the view. The highest quality optics have an image that appears pin-sharp and evenly focused across the majority of the field of view, colours that remain true to life, and bright and high light transmission qualities in low light conditions.

Test the focus wheel too. The very best binoculars have a smooth focus action that requires little movement from relatively close focus (say about five metres) all the way to infinity. Minimum focus is important too, and top-end optics can focus to within a couple of metres or so, making the close observation of insects such as butterflies and dragonflies possible.

Check the weight of a pair of binoculars and how it feels both around your neck and, more importantly, in your hands against your eyes. The way the weight is distributed can make the difference between comfort and fatigue with extended use. The best feel light in the hand, and even lighter when you rest them against your eyes.

Setting up your binoculars

Everyone is different, and all binoculars are designed to accommodate these differences. It is essential, therefore, that you set up your binoculars carefully before using them in the field to be sure of getting the best out of them.

Start by setting the eyecups. If you wear spectacles, then you are likely to want the eyecups down (bringing the glass of the exit pupil as close to your eye as possible). If not, adjust them so that the view you get is as near perfectly circular as possible when looking through one of the barrels.

Next, adjust the distance between the eyepieces. Aim to create as near a perfect circle with the view through BOTH barrels as possible (unlike the clichéd 'double barrel' view so often featured in movies when someone is looking through binoculars). Many binoculars have a scale on the centre hinge that shows you what this distance is once set, so that you can quickly return to it if they get knocked or shifted.

Now adjust the dioptre. With the vast majority of binoculars, this is on the right side and may be an adjustment ring on the eyepiece or, in some models, an adjustment within the centre focus wheel or the centre hinge section.

Start by focusing the binoculars conventionally, using the eyepiece that can only be adjusted with the conventional focus ring (usually the left). Choose an object about ten metres away so that you are not setting the binoculars' focus to infinity and focus until pin-sharp. Now close this eye and open the other eye to look through the other eyepiece, which can be adjusted with the dioptre ring. Tweak the dioptre focus so that this image is equally pin-sharp, taking care NOT to touch the main focus setting while doing this. With both eyes open, check the focus throughout the range from minimum to infinity and adjust the dioptre again if you have any doubts.

Using binoculars

Ears, eyes, binoculars – always listen and look *before* bringing binoculars into play. Scanning a scene with binoculars before having established that there is something to see often results in missing something very obvious, especially in a closed habitat such as woodland.

Once you have spotted something that warrants a closer look, it is all too easy to lose track of it as you bring the binoculars up to your eyes. To avoid this, follow these simple steps.

▶ Spot it. Look at the object you want to view more closely.

▶ Stare at it. Without looking down at your binoculars, keep your gaze fixed on the object.

▶ Bring your binoculars into your line of view. Still without shifting your gaze, bring your binoculars up into your line of view. As the image becomes clear, so it will fall directly on the subject you have been staring at. Every time!

SPOTTING SCOPES

If you develop a keen interest in the natural world, you are likely to benefit from optics with even greater magnification than a pair of binoculars generally offers – particularly if you are watching birds. This is where a telescope or spotting scope comes in. Most start at 15x magnification and may go up to 70x or 80x. Many have zoom eyepieces that allow for a range of magnifications.

All require a stout tripod or hide bracket, as the high magnifications render the scope utterly useless when hand held. Don't skimp on this element. A high-quality scope mounted on a poor-quality tripod is less use than a modest scope on a good tripod. Stability is key to a clear view.

Spotting scopes come in two main designs: with straight viewfinders or angled viewfinders. Which you opt for is down to personal choice. While many birders prefer angled eyepieces and cite comfort and low centre of gravity as drivers for their choice, I plump for the straight view. I find it simpler to 'sight' an object when looking alongside the scope barrel than when staring at an angle down at the ground. I also find the straight eyepieces easier to use in hides, for watching objects that are below the direct line of sight (such as at the base of cliffs,) and for following fast-moving objects.

Because all scopes are used with one eye (or a camera if you are digiscoping) they do not need to be adjusted for individual dioptre differences.

For pure observation, I prefer to use a scope fitted with a zoom eyepiece at its smallest magnification for the most part, as this allows for the brightest image with the widest field of view. This is especially true when 'sea watching' – using a scope from a headland to scan the open waves for pelagic seabirds such as petrels and shearwaters. I use higher magnifications when looking for detail in plumage or form – for example, when I'm watching large flocks of waders in winter plumage.

As with all the gear you are likely to need in the field, weight, durability and rugged build are all key factors to consider when choosing a scope model.

TRIPODS

As mentioned above, a good tripod is fundamental to getting clear views when using a spotting scope. It is also essential for photography, whether you are taking pictures of bugs with a macro lens or of birds with a telephoto lens. No one tripod can fulfil all applications, but there are reasonable compromises one should look for. Don't skimp on the quality of the tripod (the three legs that are your support) or the head (the bit on top of the tripod that supports your gear). When I am working with a professional video camera and telephoto lenses I invariably use a very heavy fluid head with either a steel or carbon-fibre tripod. The support rig alone weighs over ten kilograms and is massive overkill if you just want to support a spotting scope or a DSLR stills camera and telephoto lens. It also costs much more than even the top-of-the-range spotting scopes.

A light carbon-fibre tripod with a simple mechanism for hide mounting the head is ideal for most scopes and a great deal of still photography. If you intend to shoot video footage, it is important to get a tripod and head that can easily be levelled, otherwise you risk constantly sloping lakes and horizons when you pan.

Other features to look out for in a tripod are how low it can be set up, how quickly and easily its legs can be extended and collapsed, and the general durability and ruggedness of build.

NIGHT VIEWING

There are now many pieces of kit on the market designed for night observation. They come in three main technologies: infra-red lighting, thermal imaging and image intensifiers.

The cheapest by far are devices that are sensitive to infrared lighting and they are fine for medium to close observation of a subject at night. Most are in effect video cameras that are sensitive to the infrared end of the light spectrum and come with a built in IR spotlight. Because these devices need IR light (or low levels of visible light) to function, they do not work over large distances (unless a huge area is lit with IR, of course.)

Thermal imaging devices 'see' the heat profile of a scene and, depending on their level of detail, can reveal an entire landscape that is in complete darkness. When properly calibrated, they reveal warm-blooded living things as bright (or dark) objects in the scene and even the tiniest vole will stand out like a sore thumb! Thermal imaging equipment is expensive and relatively delicate, requiring constant calibration for the most effective performance.

Image intensifiers use any tiny amount of visible light (cast by stars or the moon, for example), and accelerate its energy to appear as a bright image in the device. Depending on their quality, these are really useful aids to the nocturnal observation of wildlife, but they are expensive and are limited by the need for at least some ambient light (unlike thermal imaging devices). Image intensifiers are also sensitive to infra-red light.

CAMERA GEAR

Camera equipment has undergone a rapid and exciting evolution with the advent of digital-imaging technology. The result is that even with a smart phone camera you can get high-quality images in both still and video formats.

The methods of gathering images are changing fast, but the techniques for photographing wildlife remain largely unchanged and are in effect the same as observation. The basic and most important rule remains: at no point should your attempts to get a photograph (or a view) of an animal impact negatively on your subject.

As a general rule, getting a good photograph of most British and European wild animals requires a closer view than simple observation and so the use of hides and camouflage is the norm. Getting a prolonged view of a kingfisher at 100 metres using binoculars or a spotting scope is relatively straightforward. The same species is very unlikely to sit happily three or four metres away from an observer who is not hidden, and these are the distances that allow a close clear image of a small bird.

Each species section in this book includes advice on close observation that can be applied to photography.

DIGISCOPING and DIGIBINNING

These terms describe the use of a compact digital camera in conjunction with a spotting scope or a pair of binoculars, using the optics as telephoto lenses. Digiscoping is a well-established way of recording observations with relatively inexpensive hardware. Depending on the scope you have you need to choose an appropriate digital camera and a compatible mounting rig that can be recommended by your dealer. A compact camera with an optical zoom capability of 3x or 4x is usually sufficient for this method. It's important that the object lens of the camera is roughly the same size as, or smaller than, the exit pupil of the scope or binoculars to avoid excess vignetting and light leak on to images being recorded.

I regularly use my smart phone to capture images with both my scope and my binoculars, by simply holding the lens up to the exit pupil and editing out any vignetting after the image has been taken. If the whole rig is kept relatively stable, results can be remarkably good. There are mounts available for attaching a smart phone to the eyepiece of a spotting scope, and your dealer can help with specifications.

Most smart phones are equipped with cameras, many of them very high quality. Great results can be had by holding up your phone camera to your binoculars or spotting scope, both of which can act as a telephoto lens.

CLOTHING

OUTER LAYERS

Wearing the correct clothing for wildlife watching can improve your chances of getting close, prolonged views of wild animals, and at the same time ensure you are warm, dry and comfortable at all times.

Much of the outdoor leisure industry is geared towards hiking and mountaineering, both of which encourage the use of highly visible outer layers with gaudy reflective colours. Neither of these pursuits takes into account the noise made by clothing either, and much of it comes in man-made fabrics that rustle loudly when they move.

Conversely, the hunting industry looks for precisely the same qualities required by a field naturalist when it comes to clothing. Ironic as it may seem, lots of the clothes designed for people who wish to kill animals are perfect for those who simply want to watch them at close quarters without disturbing them. A few manufacturers make clothing specifically for those who wish to observe, not kill, wildlife, notably Country Innovation in the UK.

Dull, muted and natural colours help. Camouflage clothing can be particularly useful when observing creatures with excellent eyesight, such as rural foxes and deer. Though it may be that some creatures only see in monochrome or a muted version of the colour spectrum seen by the human eye, there are those that most definitely see in colour (many birds, for example) and it helps to blend in to the world about you if at all possible.

Before you buy, test any jacket or waterproof trousers for their 'rustle factor' by rubbing the fabric against itself to hear how much sound is created. Some hunting jackets are made from wool-based fabrics, such as loden, which is all but silent when it moves, but can be heavy, and though water repellent is not waterproof.

You will undoubtedly find that the right jacket for you is a compromise between colour, rustle, waterproofing and features such as overall weight, hood, pockets and general comfort. Many of the same factors apply to trousers. I have yet to find clothing that suits all conditions and choose instead to use different outer garments, depending on the conditions and application.

If I suspect I will be observing from a kneeling position (watching otters on the coast, for example) I make sure I am wearing knee pads. Some trousers come with built-in knee protection, but any builders' merchant can supply pads, which usually fit over your trousers using a Velcro strap. These are a real life-saver when trying to walk on your knees over jagged rocks!

If you are likely to be sitting down (and you almost always will be at some point or other) a good seat-pad or cushion for your bum makes life a whole lot more comfortable than perching on a cold, damp rock or log. Again, there are many on the market – gardeners' kneeling pads do the job just fine, though I like to use a small folding pad that weighs just a few grams so is very easy to carry with me.

Be mindful of fastening types on pockets and so on. A proliferation of Velcro, for example, is a definite no-no. If you want to get something out of your pocket, and have to make a sound like ripping cotton sheets to access it, then every creature with ears will know that you are coming. Look for clothing with zips or poppers for preference.

BASE LAYERS

In cold climates you need to layer your clothing to stay warm when sitting and waiting for wildlife to show. Don't skimp on your base layers and when choosing long-sleeved vests or long johns go for good-quality fabrics with a high merino wool or silk content. These are warm, last well and wick away moisture if you sweat.

Good-quality socks, too, can keep you comfy on a cold day. I often wear a couple of pairs – a thin, close-fitting base sock that won't migrate down to my toes when I am walking, topped by an outer cashmere sock. This might sound excessive but cashmere is light, warm and wonderfully soft, as well as having superb wicking qualities.

Fleece/mid layer

I have a number of fleeces that I wear either as outer layers when conditions are dry and not too cold, or as mid layers in cold wet conditions. All are in man-made fabrics and add insulation while remaining light.

[ABOVE] There's no such thing as bad weather – only the wrong clothes! Dress warmly enough to be comfortable during a long wait.

FOOTWEAR

Conditions generally dictate which footwear is most suitable for the field naturalist. Wet, boggy ground requires a good pair of wellingtons, while dry hill country is best tackled in walking boots or shoes. I use three types of footwear.

In warm, dry environments I wear sport sandals. I prefer designs that have stout, rubber toe protection that prevents sticks, thorns and rocks from doing any damage to my toes, but still allows plenty of ventilation so my feet can breathe. Strong soles with good treads are important in a sandal too, particularly when walking in thorn country. Many are waterproof, though be aware that the insoles on some designs become hugely slippery when wet which makes them very difficult to walk in.

In dry, rough ground conditions I wear lightweight walking boots. I like boots with a good grip configuration on the sole and comfortable cushioning around the ankle.

When it comes to wellingtons, get a good quality pair. You can pick up cheap wellies from many stores, but they will lack flexibility, warmth and comfort, and since you are likely to be in wellies a lot, if you are watching wildlife in the UK or northern Europe, then it's worth splashing out (pun intended) on a good pair.

I look for wellingtons with a comfortable fit around the calf, either with an adjustable strap or neoprene upper section. They must also be flexible at the ankle and have a good grip pattern on the sole. I am often amazed at how many wellies come with nothing more than a few ridges on the sole, making them super-slippery on wet mud or grass. The best wellingtons have either a neoprene or leather lining which increases comfort and insulating properties. I have a light pair for summer and a heavier, well-insulated pair for winter. Many brands have a range of boots with different specifications and, as is so often the case, you get what you pay for.

HATS

Hats are a very personal choice and inevitably are influenced by fashion and style as well as practicality.

A wide-brimmed hat protects against both sun and rain, and has the added benefit of casting your face into shade. A shaded face stands out less; an asset when trying to watch keen-eyed creatures. The latter also applies to peaked caps, which are ideal for sunny days. Both of these styles can compromise the use of larger cameras, as the brim or peak pushes against the back of the camera before you can get your eye to the eyepiece. You can reverse them but risk looking a little odd! In colder weather, I wear a beanie-style insulating hat and I have a particular favourite that is hand-knitted from Shetland wool.

BALACLAVAS and SCARVES

In really cold conditions, face and neck protection is a must, and has the bonus of camouflaging pale skin. I rarely use full-face balaclavas, finding that even the best of them affect my peripheral vision negatively, but I often use neck protectors. The best of these are versatile tubes of fabric that can be used as scarves, hats, face covers and even lens camouflage! Buff make a wide range.

FIELD SENSE

Many wild animals are armed with a battery of senses that are constantly tuned to be on the alert for a meal or, conversely, to avoid becoming a meal! Regardless of our intentions, we are regarded as a mortal danger by most of these creatures. This is hardly surprising, given our species' history of persecuting wild animals, and as a result most avoid us like the plague. If you are going to get good views of nervous wild animals, you must learn to understand their senses and act accordingly.

SMELL – READING THE WIND

Lots of mammals (and a few bird species) have an exceptionally keen sense of smell. Just watch a well-trained dog sniffing out a favourite toy or following the trail of another animal and you realise how phenomenal a sense of smell can be, especially when compared to our own dulled abilities. This does mean that to many animals, humans stink – regardless of how well washed you might be!

There are ways of camouflaging your scent with varying degrees of efficacy. You can purchase clothing lined with activated carbon and other products that absorb some of the scent that emanates from your body. Having used these products I find that while they may reduce the human smell, they can't eliminate it, especially when you consider that every time you exhale, your breath will carry scent. Even activated carbon face masks are fallible, and short of using a full-body biohazard suit (hardly suitable for comfortable wildlife watching), it is virtually

impossible to trap all your body aromas. There are also commercially available sprays and creams that are designed to mask your scent with another, more pungent smell. I have field-tested a number of these products and found none of them to be any more effective than simply rubbing some fresh earth over my bare skin – and to be honest, even this has little or no effect.

In my opinion, rather than trapping or masking your smell, it is far better to ensure your scent does not pass over the nose of a wild animal in the first place.

This requires an acute and constant sense of wind direction. Some naturalists (and many hunters) carry a small bag or tub of cornflour or powdered chalk and sprinkle some into the air to determine the wind direction and the path it takes. However, any walk in the wilds is likely to provide a natural alternative to these powders and these vary depending on the weather conditions and time of year. In spring, dandelion seeds become perfect little airborne parachutes that show not only the wind direction but also all its twists and swirls as it passes over land forms and through trees. At other times of year, a dried leaf, crumbled in the hand, or the seeds from a willow catkin, willow herb or thistle all do the same job.

By and large, an awareness of the wind based on observing how vegetation responds to its drift, or the feeling of it on your face or other bare skin, should be enough to inform you of its general direction and guide you to move through the landscape accordingly. If I am intending to watch an animal with a keen sense of smell,

my first task is always to determine the wind direction, so that I can plan my approach. This is especially important when watching otters, badgers, foxes and deer species.

Our own sense of smell is pretty basic when compared to that of many other creatures. That said, it can still be a very useful sense for the field naturalist. Many mammals use scent to mark their territory and some of these 'calling cards' are perceptible to the human nose. Details of these can be found under each species heading where relevant.

Also, a decaying corpse has a very distinctive and powerful smell, and this can lead you to an area where a predator has been active or scavengers may be present.

SIGHT
Hide your form

The pros and cons of using camouflage clothing are dealt with on pages 22–23, but even if you do not blend entirely into the landscape, having an awareness of your surroundings and behaving accordingly can play a huge part in remaining undetected by the sharp eyes of your wild subject. For starters, keep still. I find it astonishing how a person can remain undetected, even if wearing bright colours, as long as they do not move. This may be partly due to the fact that many animals, particularly mammals, have only limited perception of the full colour spectrum. But even to human eyes – which in common with those of other primates are well tuned to colour – a static human form is much less eye-catching than a moving one, regardless of the colour of the clothing.

If you are staying still, either seated or standing, then try to use vegetation or land forms to break up your outline. Keep your back to a tree or bush, sit low on a bank, or lie flat in a sand dune. Strike a compromise between remaining well hidden and maintaining a good view. With creatures that are likely to be lower than your viewing position, such as otters on the coast, consider their point of view and how you may appear to them. You may find that

[ABOVE] Always consider the point of view of the animal you are trying to observe. If your outline stands out against the sky you are far more likely to disturb your intended subject. Keep a low profile to avoid detection.

you need to retreat to a point against a high bank to prevent your silhouette from breaking the skyline. Even if a small part of your body, such as your head, is in stark relief against the sky, it may be enough to catch the eye of an otter and startle it.

It's important to pay attention to the light conditions too. Dappled sunlight in a woodland creates a broken patchwork of bright areas and darker shade which can cloak your form. Low, direct sunlight reveals every detail of the human outline, and highlights any bare skin, especially if you are Caucasian and pale. If wind conditions allow, having the prevailing light behind you or off to one side makes it easier to blend in with your surroundings.

HOW TO WALK

Odd though it may seem, the way in which you move dramatically affects your chances

of seeing wild animals. For inspiration, watch a roe deer moving through a woodland. Every step is placed gingerly on the vegetation; each move is followed by a pause and careful scrutiny of sound and scent. To be part of this wild world, adopt a similar strategy, even if you are not aware of there being any creatures nearby that may be watching you.

A normal human walking gait, in traditional walking shoes or boots, is a heavy-footed affair. We fall on to each foot with a thud and disregard the effect we have

[ABOVE] Use any available cover to break up your outline and try to keep your face in shade whenever possible.

[RIGHT] Walk to the side of a muddy path, rather than on it, to preserve sign left by creatures that have gone before you.

on any vegetation underfoot. Learn to hear the consequence of your movement and adapt your pace and footfall accordingly. 'Feel' your way along a woodland path, slowly and deliberately controlling your pace and footfall so that you are in control the whole time. If you feel a stick beneath your foot, adjust your step to prevent it snapping. Ironically, if you were to walk through the woods in bare feet, you would do this naturally. Indeed, if you run in bare feet, you instinctively land on the ball of your foot rather than your heel, allowing your Achilles tendon to act as a shock absorber rather than your knees taking the full brunt of the force.

As well as remaining alert for wildlife, keep an eye on the track ahead. Watch for sticks or dry leaves that may be noisy if stood on, and scan for animal tracks and sign. If you spot an area of exposed soil on the track, avoid walking directly on it so that you don't disturb any footprints that may have been left there.

'DISINTERESTED' OBSERVATION

The way you move once you have spotted a wild creature also affects the your chance of a prolonged and clear view. For example, imagine you are walking through a woodland edge and while scanning, you notice a roe deer watching you from cover some 20 metres away to the right. Your instinct is to stop, turn to face the deer and look directly at it. As a result you will almost certainly send it running off in alarm. Many wild animals will watch you from a distance if they do not think they have been spotted, and you must keep them believing that this is the case.

Let's imagine you are aware that there is a deer watching you, but rather than turning to face it you continue to walk slowly, and turn your face in the opposite direction. You can turn back briefly to note the deer's position, but try to avoid facing it directly. Be aware of the spot the deer is occupying in the wood and either stake out a likely point at which it may emerge into the open – a field border, for instance – or move away completely and then approach from a different direction, bearing in mind all the elements that may give you away. With this new, stealthy approach to movement you will hear and see a great deal more.

HOW TO LISTEN

If you are lucky enough to be able to hear well, you have a tool that will open the wild world and offer manifold chances of encounters with charismatic creatures.

A strong knowledge of the 'language' of the wild is undoubtedly key to spotting and understanding wildlife, but this is something that can only be developed with time and field experience. This language is not restricted to vocalisations, but also includes mechanical sounds and the effect a creature has on its neighbours. Alarm calls, for example, can provide you with a clue that not only is there a predator in the area, but also which species that predator may be.

The more you become familiar with this natural symphony, the more you will become a part of the wild world you want to witness.

Some sounds in nature are very soft or else have a ventriloquial quality. You can pinpoint these sounds by ear-cupping. It may seem like a bit of nonsense, but cupping your hands behind your ears really does

help to home in on the direction of a sounds like those made by a churring nightjar or a singing grasshopper warbler. For some high-pitched sounds this increases your chance of hearing them clearly by reducing the white noise coming into your ears from all directions.

ALARM CALLS

As mentioned above, the alarm calls of creatures that have sensed danger are a wonderful aid to wildlife observation. This is true the world over, from the African savannah, where zebra and topi wheeze and snort their alarm on seeing a lion, to the back gardens of Britain. Learning these calls and the subtlety of tone that can inform you not only of the presence of a predator but also its species, takes time and field experience. Below are some likely pairs of predator and prey to listen and look out for.

[ABOVE] Many animals make alarm calls when they spot a predator, and these calls may be species specific or at least give you a good idea of the type of predator that is the cause of the disturbance. Grey squirrels, for example, call incessantly if they spot a resting fox.

Blackbird/Tawny owl
A blackbird facing into an ivy-clad tree, producing a loud and metallic 'pin-pink-pink' call is strong evidence of a roosting tawny owl.

Blue tit/Sparrowhawk
Blue, great and long-tailed tits all produce very high-pitched, discordant whistles of alarm when they spot a fast-moving bird of prey. These are often the first clues you get that a sparrowhawk is nearby.

House martin/Hobby
House martins and swallows are both attacked from time to time by hobbies. Their alarm calls when they spot this fast-moving falcon are very distinctive.

Grey squirrel/Fox
Squirrels may alarm call at roosting owls, but are more likely to produce their wheezing repetitive 'chuck-chuck-chuck-wheeeeze' when they spot trouble on the ground. This may be a domestic cat, but the call may also be a sign that squirrels have spotted a fox resting in the undergrowth.

THE AGES OF HEARING

As animal hearing capacity goes, we humans are pretty average. We can hear neither very low (infra) sounds nor very high (ultra) sounds. The animal kingdom is peppered with many examples of creatures whose hearing is either more sensitive or covers a wider range than our own.

The typical range cited for human hearing is 20–20,000 Hz. The bigger the number, the higher the sound. As we age, most of us slowly lose some hearing capacity, especially in the higher frequencies, and so some elements of the natural world are lost to us too.

As a kid, I would often listen to noctule bats heading out to feed high over the suburban gardens of Bristol, and the leaf litter in my local woodland twittered and squeaked with the shrill voices of common and pigmy shrews. Now I find that I cannot hear these sounds, and I miss them hugely. It was once so easy to pinpoint a high-flying noctule through its calls alone, or to stop and listen to a hunting shrew. Now I must depend on my eyes alone, or pick up the mechanical sounds created by the animals' movements. Alternatively, I can use technology in the form of a bat detector (page 167). That said, I am still able (aged 52) to pick up some key high-pitched sounds such as kingfisher calls, lower-frequency vole squeaks and goldcrest twittering.

HOW TO LOOK

Looking and seeing are very different things. As our ancestors moved around, their eyes would have been constantly scanning for food or danger, with occasional diversions driven by the desire to mate.

Anyone can look at the ground. Only some people will see the faint claw marks in the soil that betray the passing of a badger in the night. We can all walk through a woodland with our gaze drifting over the surrounding tree trunks and tangle of vegetation, but only a few of us will see the roe deer, stock still in the midst of it.

Learning to use your eyes to see what is around you is perhaps one of the most important and basic skills of fieldcraft and wildlife watching. With very few exceptions, we can all do it.

Learn to see

Learn to respond instantly to the subtlest of sounds by allowing your gaze to be drawn in the direction of any noise that catches your attention. The snap of a twig, the rustle of a leaf, a gentle twittering in the treetops above, should all command your visual interest.

Learn to be patient. Many wild creatures are masters of disguise and it can be very tricky to pick out their form in the midst of their environment. To find the source of a sound, watch the spot the sound seems to emanate from closely.

Predictive vision

If you spot a sensitive wild creature before it spots you, you stand a much better chance of getting a prolonged view of it.

By training yourself to look through multiple planes the whole time, you cover much more of your environment and accordingly stand a better chance of seeing things before they see you. As well as looking for immediate signs close to where you are walking, keep checking the middle and far distance of the route you intend to take. Don't forget to look left, right and – from time to time – behind you. Many is the time I have moved through a wood or field, only to turn around carefully to find I am being watched by a deer or other creature that has allowed me to pass.

Search image

If you keep in your mind's eye the creatures you are hoping to see, then you are more likely to spot them. There is nothing mystical about this (in my opinion), but the simple fact is that if your thoughts are prepared to witness a form, then your eyes distinguish that form in the environment more readily. It is really no different from recognising the face of a friend in a crowd of people. If you are looking for frogs along a pond margin, then you will ignore most shapes unless they resemble a frog. If you are looking for hares huddled in fields, then the russet colour and hunched hind quarters will catch your eye at quite a distance if you are already 'thinking hare'. Of course, familiarity with the form through first-hand

experience helps enormously and makes it more likely that you will recognise the sometimes very subtle glimpses of a creature that doesn't wish to be spotted.

Heading out with a strong search image does have its disadvantages. Recently I went to watch brown hares on an island off the west coast of Scotland. Much of the habitat the hares occupied was along the coastal strip and I was able to scour the fields on the landward side of the coastal road and find many hares. The same stretch of coastline was perfect otter habitat, but I didn't see a single otter during my stay for the simple reason that I wasn't looking for them. My attention was focused 100 per cent on the fields and hills, not on the coastal rocks or water. It is very likely I passed by a number of otters during my trip, and never saw a single one.

For the most part, you will be looking for whatever catches your eye though, and the more search images you develop, the more likely you are to encounter these creatures without having to focus on them.

Peripheral vision

Many people refer to having a sixth sense. 'I just had the feeling I was being watched' is a phrase I have often heard when being told of a close encounter with a wild animal.

It is my firm belief that we all have this sense, but there is nothing mystical about it. Instead it is an extension of our existing senses – sight, hearing and smell – to which we are not attuned but we still respond. Peripheral vision is one of these.

Test the limits of your peripheral vision by holding your fingers out at arm's length while staring straight ahead. You may be surprised at how far you can see to the side.

The area of our eye's retina that can resolve a well-defined image is very small indeed. Just fix your stare on this dot . and notice that the words 'dot' and 'and' are both out of focus. You can see them, but not as clearly as you can see the dot. If the gaps between the dot and the words were much larger, you wouldn't be able to read the words on either side of it. When we look at the world about us, we are constantly scanning the scene with our eyes and moving our head to accommodate as wide an area as possible. Our brain does a super job of building up a picture of the whole, despite the fact the image is made up of thousands of tiny 'windows' and slices. If something 'catches our eye' it is working outside the narrow area of clear focus, and demanding our attention. We can't help but respond by moving our eyes or head (or both) to get a clear image.

In a moment go back to staring at the dot on the page (or anything else) but this time stretch your arms out to the side and stick your forefingers up in the air. Still staring at the point ahead of you, very slowly bring your arms forwards, but be aware of the moment you pick up any movement created by your outstretched arms and fingers. You may well be surprised how little you have to move your arms before you spot your hands. In my case, I have a peripheral vision arc of about 178 degrees, which is very nearly a semicircle. Of course, the detail and resolution of these peripheral views is very poor, but the movement is most definitely visible. The more responsive you are to your peripheral vision the more you will see. This is especially true as the light fades.

The retina is covered with two different types of light-sensitive cell, known as rods and cones. The most numerous are the rods;

Developing a search image for a species you are looking for is often the key to success. Having the shape and colour of a resting hare [ABOVE LEFT] or a roe deer in woodland [ABOVE RIGHT] in your mind's eye will help you pick out the most cryptic of forms.

there are about 120 million of them in each eye. By comparison, there are only about six or seven million cones, and most of these are concentrated in our visual hot spot, known as the macula – the bit that you were using when focusing on the dot. Cones give us our wonderful colour vision (and, by the way, we are pretty good at seeing colour compared to most of the rest of the animal kingdom), while the rods are more sensitive to light. As it gets darker, coloured light is in short supply and the central portion of our vision begins to fade and fail. Our rods, meanwhile, are still doing a pretty good job. The trouble is, most of us take little or no notice of this!

If you are in a dark space, try hard to concentrate on your peripheral vision. The temptation is to look towards any movement or form that catches your eye, but if you resist this urge you will see better than if you were to look directly at it. It takes a bit of getting used to, but with practice you can train your eyes (and brain) to see pretty well in the dark.

THE ART OF CONCEALMENT

There are a number of creatures with eyesight and powers of perception so great that they will sometimes spot you even when you are wearing neutral colours and remain completely still. These include foxes (those in rural areas, which have an understandable fear of humans) and most deer species.

Camouflage

Camouflage can make the difference between having prolonged, close views of these animals, or none at all. You only have to look to the natural world for inspiration. Many creatures have evolved to blend in with their environment, either to hide from predators – for example, a nightjar resting on the ground where it blends almost perfectly with its surroundings – or to avoid detection by prey, like a leopard whose spotted coat makes it hard to see. There are also animals that can adapt their camouflage to suit their environment, including frogs, cuttlefish and several species of flatfish.

Most natural camouflage patterns have some features in common, regardless of the environment they have evolved to blend in with. Among these is disruptive patterning – cryptic pale and dark shapes alongside one another. The eye is drawn to the highlights and the brain links these with other bright patches in the immediate surroundings without associating them with the adjacent dark areas, thus breaking up the outline of the creature.

For example, a ringed plover standing on a plain surface, such as a tarmac road, seems brightly coloured and poorly camouflaged, with its sandy-coloured back, brilliant white belly and stark black banding across its breast and through its eye. However, the very same bird sitting on its nest in full view but on a beach strewn with light and dark pebbles, is all but invisible, courtesy of the disruptive pattern of light and dark plumage.

There are myriad commercially available camouflage patterns available on everything from jackets and trousers (as you might expect) to underwear and armchairs! Most of these are designed as much to appeal to the human eye as they are to camouflage your outline, and some are more versatile than others. That said, no single pattern works effectively in all habitats. A woodland pattern may help you blend in among trees, but you will still stand out like a sore thumb

in the middle of a grassy field. A snow pattern has both obvious advantages and limitations, depending on the amount of surrounding snow cover.

Ideally you choose, or create, your camouflage according to your environment and the conditions on the day. My default choices for clothing colours are neutral earth tones (greens and browns) and I use available vegetation to add to these if I want to break up my outline further. On occasion I use full camouflage or even a ghillie suit, which can work well if I plan to remain in one place for extended periods.

Hides

The most effective way to hide the human form is, as the name suggests, a hide, known as a blind in the United States. Many reserves are equipped with public hides – substantial wooden buildings where the visitor can sit comfortably and watch the nearby wildlife without disturbing it.

The basic principle of any hide is simple: viewing windows are small and the interior is darker than the world outside. Anything within the hide is hidden by shade in contrast to the glare of light on the outside, and most, if not all, of the human form is hidden from view. Keeping the interior of a hide dark is key to its efficacy, which is why it is important to close the shutters on observation windows when you leave a public hide, and to open the door briefly and close it swiftly and as quietly as possible as you enter and leave.

Great views can be had of a wide variety of creatures from this type of hide, but for

[ABOVE] Ghillie suits were developed for the armed forces, but they work equally well to camouflage the human form when watching wildlife.

more targeted observation and photography, a portable hide is the answer. There are many models available, some of which are designed specifically for observation and photography, while others are made with shooting in mind. Look for a design that has versatile windows (with large and small openings) on at least three sides, ideally with a secondary netting window cover. This acts in the same way as net curtains in the window of a house, preventing prying eyes seeing beyond the bright netting and into the dark interior. When choosing a portable hide, ease of set up and break down are worth consideration too, as is overall construction quality.

When using a portable hide to watch or photograph an animal away from its den or nest, it is usually fine to set it up and wait for the creature's return without a lengthy introduction period. An example may be a spot near to a branch overhanging a pond or river that is regularly used by a kingfisher as a hunting perch.

To use a hide to observe or photograph birds at the nest or mammals at a breeding or resting den, a more careful introduction is required. Before considering any such approach, check the law concerning the subject you hope to watch. Many species are protected by law, and wilful disturbance of these can result in hefty fines at the very least, not to mention the more lasting impact of negatively affecting the breeding success of the creature you are trying to watch.

In England, Scotland, Wales and Northern Ireland lists of protected species and appropriate photographic licensing procedures are available online. Regardless of the legal status of the species you hope to watch, extreme care must be taken so as not to have a negative impact on the animal. Details of how each species should be approached are covered in the relevant sections.

If you don't have a portable hide you can use locally available materials to build a temporary structure that serves as a field hide – a screen behind which you can sit to watch wildlife that is likely to return to the area to feed, socialise or breed. These structures are especially useful when watching woodland or woodland edge creatures, such as badgers, foxes and most deer species.

There is no one method for building a field hide. Almost any structure will do the trick, but starting with an existing feature or vegetation, such as an old stone wall or a large tree, gives you the foundations and ensures that your outline is unlikely to catch the eye of the creatures you are watching.

A typical field hide construction is illustrated opposite. Pay attention to the side views as well as the view from the front of the hide, since a deer or fox is just as likely to approach from this angle as any other.

[LEFT] Portable hides come in many designs but all shroud the human shape from the eyes of creatures that perceive us as a mortal threat.

[RIGHT] Field hides can be built with any available material. Make sure the base structure is self supporting before covering it with local vegetation.

THE
WILDLIFE

MAMMALS 28 | BIRDS 182

REPTILES 232 | AMPHIBIANS 238

INVERTEBRATES 244

RED FOX *Vulpes vulpes*

SIGN
FOOTPRINTS
Small dogs and foxes leave tracks that are superficially similar. Both have four toes on each foot and both usually reveal claw marks. Large dogs can be ruled out due to size alone, but even the tracks of dogs with feet of a similar size to a fox lack certain key features of a fox print.

Fox tracks, especially those created by the rear feet, are teardrop shaped as opposed to oval like a dog's. This is because the two middle toes are of equal length and usually held close together, while the outer two toes fall well short of the middle pair. A dog's middle toes tend to be more splayed and of slightly unequal length, with the outer toes much closer to the same length as the middle pair. Most dogs also have a heel pad that is larger in relation to the toes than a fox's.

A clear fox track reveals a distinctive 'X' shape through the centre, created by the symmetrical positioning of the small heel pad, outer toes and tightly held inner toes (see below). In perfect conditions, the fine hair between the pads leaves an impression.

Foxes tend to leave their tracks in what appears to be a straight line. At walking pace, a fox frequently steps into the print left by its front foot with its rear foot, and with

SIZE
Weight: 2.5–15kg
Length to rump: 45–90cm
Tail length: 32–53cm
Height at shoulder: 35–50cm

Front left print (actual size)

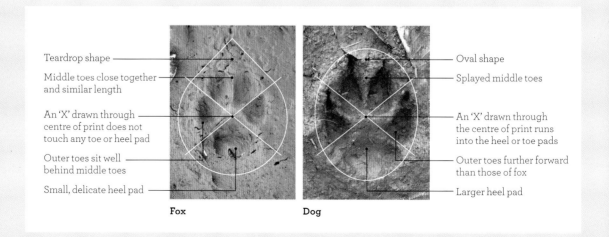

Teardrop shape

Middle toes close together and similar length

An 'X' drawn through centre of print does not touch any toe or heel pad

Outer toes sit well behind middle toes

Small, delicate heel pad

Oval shape

Splayed middle toes

An 'X' drawn through the centre of print runs into the heel or toe pads

Outer toes further forward than those of fox

Larger heel pad

Fox   **Dog**

indistinct prints this can make the whole footprint look larger than it truly is.

In snow, fox tracks follow a typically wavering path as the animal checks out various opportunities to get a meal, sniffing a grass tuft here, listening to a vole moving there. Foxes can hear voles moving in their runs even through very deep snow and will leap into the air before stuffing their head and muzzle down through the snow at the point where they think the vole is walking in an attempt to catch it. Such hunting behaviour leaves very distinctive marks in the snow. While marking their territory, both male and female foxes urinate on features such as grass tussocks, and the resulting yellowing of the snow is obvious and distinctive.

A typical overprint – the fox has stepped with its rear foot on the print made by its front foot.

FAECES *Scat or droppings*

The colour and shape of fox scat varies enormously. This reflects the animal's very broad tastes in food, which may range from their staple diet of small mammals, birds and earthworms, to berries and nuts. Where foxes have access to human food waste, predominantly in urban areas, they happily feast on anything from fried chicken to pizza! The resulting form, colour and texture of the scats may vary from those full of hair or well-compacted feathers to others made up almost entirely of soil when earthworms have been the major food item. Scat containing small mammal hair tends to be 5–8cm long, twisted and with tapering ends. If the fox has been eating loose material, such as earthworms or berries, the scats may look very like those of a dog, but are more slender and elongated than most.

Foxes often leave scat on prominent features, such as molehills and grass tufts. The upper image shows typical scat excreted after eating earthworms. The scat in the lower image contains feathers and mammal hair.

A distinctive feature of fox scat is where you find it. Foxes usually leave their faeces in prominent places, such as in the middle of a track or on a tuft of grass or rock. Dogs, however, usually 'drop where they stop' rather than picking out a prominent feature in the landscape. Of course, responsible dog owners collect their pet's faeces and remove them from the landscape altogether.

The scent of fox scat is pungent. While the base scent varies depending on the diet, there is usually a hint of the fox's own scent as a top note. A rather more pure form of this 'fox scent' is present in the fox's urine, and is detectable by most human noses even at a distance.

In areas where rabbits are common, foxes often target them as a mainstay of their diet, especially when they are rearing cubs.

Describing scent is notoriously tricky, but I rather like the smell of fox, which has a sweet top note, with heavy musk base notes. It may be described as violets and sandalwood, or rose water with aniseed and musk. Once you get your 'nose in', any walk through the countryside or along a city street will be punctuated by waves of fox whiff you pass through! From the fox's point of view, the real purpose of its scent is for marking territory.

FEEDING SIGNS

After most meals there is little or no sign that a fox has been feeding. Mice and voles are devoured whole, as are small birds, earthworms, beetles and bugs.

Foxes eat a lot of earthworms and in the right warm, damp conditions hardly leave a mark where they grab and pull up their wiggly snacks. Sometimes though, foxes dig a little where they believe a worm has disappeared beneath the surface, leaving shallow, often slightly fan-shaped scrapes with clear claw marks here and there. They may also stuff their muzzle into a tangle of grass and soft earth to grab a worm or beetle grub, and this action leaves a narrow, slightly fan-shaped impression on the grass and soil.

When hunting for voles or earthworms in long grass, a fox will often leave 'snuff-holes'. These are roughly triangular in form, reflecting the shape of the fox's muzzle.

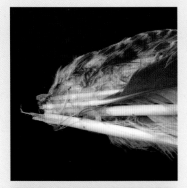

A fox uses its carnassial teeth to shear the flight and tail feathers of larger birds from their carcass. The quills bear neat cuts along their base and are often clumped together, especially if they originate from the bird's 'wrist'.

Back or belly hair may be snagged on a wire fence, depending on its height. Back hair (above) is reddish-brown and belly hair grey-white. Both have a very fine, fluffy texture.

Rabbits are a common food item for foxes and they may be eaten whole when very young, but more usually the feet, intestines and some skin are left behind. Rabbit bones that have been shattered near the foot, with the meatless skin of the upper leg and thigh still attached, are a sign that a fox has been at work. Foxes wipe their faces clean of fur along the ground on nearby grass, and clumps of rabbit fur stuck on the grass and held together with the saliva of a fox are another good clue. On a warm day the saliva will dry and may look a little like the slime left by a slug or snail.

When a fox kills and eats larger birds, such as wood pigeons, it usually plucks the breast feathers first, using its incisor teeth to clean its meal. The fox discards these small feathers by shaking its head or running its tongue through its incisor teeth, so the feathers may scatter over a wide area, especially if there has been a breeze. If the fox cannot dislodge a clump of feathers from its mouth in this manner, it may rub its face on the ground, leaving clumps of small feathers bound together with saliva. Wing feathers are sheared off using the carnassial teeth (the scissor-like teeth at the back of the jaw), and a clean cut along the base of several primary or secondary feathers that remain clumped together is another clear sign that a fox has been feeding.

Foxes may also eat the eggs of ground-nesting birds and break the shell with a bite. They lick up the contents (or extract the developing embryo), leaving eggshell remains and often some of the albumen on the ground.

Foxes also eat blackberries with alacrity, though they can only reach those on the lowest branches of the bush. You may, rarely, find tufts of fox hair snagged on the lowest prickles of a blackberry bush and these are a sign of this feeding behaviour.

HAIR

Where foxes encounter wire fences or other obstacles, they may leave tufts of hair – from their belly on very low snags, or from their back if they push underneath a fence. Fox hair is fine and soft. Belly hair is greyish or off-white and back hair is anything from ginger brown to yellow buff. Some of the guard hairs have a dark, blackish tip. The grey, fluffy undercoat rarely gets snagged on obstacles, though small

[ABOVE LEFT] As fox cubs grow and venture beyond the entrance to the earth, they crush the surrounding vegetation as they play. Here, the stems of bluebells have been flattened, and the cubs' direction of travel back into the earth entrance is clear from the lie of the stems that have been worn flat and line the hole.

[ABOVE RIGHT] Where there is little or no vegetation, wear around the earth entrance is more subtle but still apparent from the worn soil and scratch marks.

amounts may be present along with the longer, coarser guard hairs. The hair feels very fine and soft, and can be rolled easily between finger and thumb (Badger page 42).

HOME

In fine weather, foxes prefer to rest above ground. In urban areas the chosen spot may be a shed roof or the edge of a quiet flower border. In more rural areas any patch of cover that allows the fox the opportunity to rest well and make a hasty exit if necessary will do. Places like the base of blackthorn thicket or a sunny patch adjacent to thick bramble bushes are favourites. I have even seen foxes sleeping in the boles of pollarded willows and the forked branches of apple trees, well over two metres off the ground. A favourite daybed may be used repeatedly and result in a worn, shallow bowl made by the curled body of the animal. Look out for shed hair and check the scent in these couches.

During inclement weather foxes take to cover. This may be any natural (or unnatural) shelter, from rocky overhangs and hollow logs to a space beneath a garden shed.

When expecting a family, the vixen seeks out or digs an earth – a sheltered and peaceful den. This may be dug directly into loose soil from scratch (excuse the pun) or she may use and extend existing burrow systems (such as rabbit warrens or badger setts). In man-made environments, the areas beneath garden sheds are a favourite, but I have seen urban fox dens in cavities in walls (where bricks are missing or airbricks have shattered to allow access) and in piles of pallets or tyres in rubbish tips.

There may be very little sign of activity around an earth when the cubs are very young but as they mature, the area grows progressively more worn and messy. There may be little scats here and there, and food remains that have been used as playthings. Anything from bird wings and the feet of roe deer fawns to rubber balls and chewed shoes may show up! The most active earth entrance may have very worn vegetation around its entire periphery.

HOW TO WATCH

Equipped with a first-class battery of senses, foxes can be tricky or easy to watch, depending on their experiences of encountering humans. In rural areas, where there has been a long history of persecution from people, foxes are among the most timid and difficult to watch of all British wild mammals. But in urban areas, where they are regularly exposed to benign or even friendly humans, they may be remarkably confident, even approaching certain people with whom they are very familiar.

Even where foxes are used to humans, it is important to consider the type of exposure they have been used to. In inner cities, such as London, Bristol or Glasgow, all of which have large urban fox populations, foxes may appear remarkably tame, but if you behave 'oddly' they quickly become suspicious and slip away. Like all wild animals they vary enormously from one individual to the next. In one London garden, we have documentary evidence of a vixen remaining calm and snoozing on a shed roof even when people are in the garden, while another fox in the same community slips away into cover the moment there is the slightest hint of a person opening the back door.

When watching foxes in the city, try to seem as indifferent as possible. It is often better to talk quietly rather than remain silent in their presence (humans are noisy beasts and a silent one is suspicious!) If you see a fox, do not stare directly at it (see 'disinterested' observation page 17).

With time and patience, urban foxes can learn to accept a human at remarkably close quarters, though I would not advocate hand feeding a wild fox. While it is possible to nurture this level of trust, it does not do the fox any favours,

Mating: December/January

Gestation: 49–58 days

Young: 2–12 cubs (usually 5 or 6) cubs born February/March

Emergence of young: cubs usually appear above ground in mid-April

Foxes are remarkably good climbers and may rest several metres above the ground on shed roofs, the tops of walls or in trees.

sending a message that all humans may be prepared to do the same thing and creating the very real risk of a hostile encounter between a fearful human, fox, or both!

Trying to watch a rural fox is a whole different ballgame. Having suffered a legacy of persecution from sheep and poultry farmers, gamekeepers and, it seems at times, just about everyone with a bit of land to their name, rural foxes have learned to shun the company of humans. Those that do not are rarely long for this world. To watch rural foxes successfully you must pay attention to every potential cue that you are in the area – wind direction, outline, movement and sound (pages 14–17). Foxes are among the few creatures that frequently look up when they are foraging, so even an elevated position may not be safe for undisturbed observation. I have often built local material field hides or worn ghillie suits (page 23) to watch, photograph and film rural foxes. The only exception to this style of observation, which allows for the widest possible field of view, is when the foxes have young and the breeding earth may be staked out using a portable hide. Wind direction remains important of course (foxes can still smell you even if they can't see you), as does the gradual introduction of the hide over three or four days (page 24).

Weather permitting, fox cubs aged between four and eight weeks follow a remarkably consistent activity cycle over the whole of the UK, and, where undisturbed, elsewhere in the rest of their very wide range. While they are sporadically busy through the hours of darkness, daylight activity frequently occurs at about 8.00, 14.00 and again shortly before dusk (in April and May about 20.00). This is, of course, reliant on fair weather, and rain will stop or delay play. Foxes, especially young ones, don't like getting wet!

Take care not to make a single sound if a fox stares in your direction, and this includes the taking of photographs. It is far better to wait for the animal to relax and look away than risk spooking it for the sake of an image. Fox body language is relatively easy to read since so much of it is similar to that of a domestic dog. An alert fox focuses, wide eyed, with ears trained on the source of its concern. A relaxed animal will be scanning with ears frequently swivelling in different directions and eyes in a more relaxed, even half-closed mode.

FOX SENSES

Sound	Sight	Smell
8	5	10

Over much of their range and for most of the year, foxes are predominantly nocturnal. They use their finely honed range of senses to detect their food as well as any signs of danger.

Only when an animal is in this latter state should you consider taking a photograph or moving in any way that may betray your presence.

Many fox breeding earths are situated where thick cover meets an open area. This gives the adults the opportunity to scan the area for danger from a distance before approaching. It also gives the young cubs the choice of playing in the safety of the thicket or careering around in the open. Only in the quietest rural spots is the latter likely to occur on a regular basis in daylight, but where it does, it offers the opportunity to observe the fox family with few obstacles blocking the view. If you are considering introducing a hide to a field, extend the length of time you take to introduce it to six to eight days. Some adult foxes will consider moving their litter if they feel they are being watched!

Foxes respond to certain sounds by coming closer to investigate. This trait has long been used by those who have a mind to shoot them, but the technique can also be useful for the benign wildlife enthusiast who wants a close look at these exquisite creatures. There are two categories of mimicry that may pique the interest of a fox: that of a fellow fox, or its prey.

Perhaps the best known fox-luring call is the rabbit distress squeal. There are commercially available whistles that can produce the sound, usually comprising a reed pulled taut in a narrow gap that vibrates when you blow across it – much as one can hold a blade of grass between your thumbs to the same effect. However, it is perfectly possible to create the sound with just your lips and hand. Make a tube by curling your fingers and thumb, as though you were holding a narrow pole. Now bring your hand to your mouth, and with your lips against the hole made by your thumb and forefinger, produce a kissing sound. With practice you can make a lifelike squeal, with the wavering elements of the sound created by wobbling your hand to vary the pitch.

This only attracts foxes that live in areas where rabbits are a common food item. Elsewhere, mimicking a vole squeaking (page 186) can bring a fox trotting up for a closer look.

Foxes mate during the months of December and January in northern Europe and it is then that they are at their most vocal. Screams, cackles and barks are all part of the symphony. One call described as the 'wow-wow' bark is particularly associated with this time of year and with practice a human voice can produce a reasonable impression of it. I use the falsetto range of my voice and utter three or four 'wows' in quick succession. The 'wow-wow' bark can attract both dog and vixen fox, but only during this narrow window in the year.

BADGER *Meles meles*

SIGN

FOOTPRINTS

Badgers leave a characteristic footprint that has a 'square' overall shape.

A clear front footprint shows five evenly spaced forward-facing toes that run in a slight arc around the leading edge of the heel pad. Each toe leads to a long, straight claw mark (usually separated from the toe pad by at least 5mm).

A clear rear footprint is similar in form to the front print, though smaller and with far less pronounced claw marks.

The heel pad on both front and rear prints is solid looking, with an arced, rectangular kidney shape.

On harder ground, badgers may leave nothing more than a few claw marks but even these, with their even spacing and fairly parallel alignment, are distinctive.

Badgers are significantly less active during the cold winter months than at other times of year. With their favourite food of earthworms unavailable, they prefer to snooze away much of the hard weather. That said, they do not hibernate as such and will venture out even when thick snow is on the ground if they are hungry and in search of a meal. On crisp snow, their footprints show well, but in wet or powder snow much of the definition may be lost. The prints can still be identified, though, by their square form

SIZE
Weight: 7–15kg
Length to rump: about 75cm
Tail length: about 15cm
Height at shoulder: 30cm

Front right print (actual size)

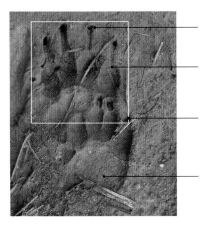

Long, powerful claw marks (longer on front feet)

Five toes, close together in a slight curve around heel pad

'Square' form to print

Kidney-shaped heel pad

[OPPOSITE TOP] Badgers are almost exclusively nocturnal in their habits, but in places where they are undisturbed they may venture above ground well before sunset.

[OPPOSITE BOTTOM LEFT] Prints in deep, wet mud lack defined toe marks but still bear the square form and deep claw marks that characterise them.

[OPPOSITE BOTTOM RIGHT] Badgers are creatures of habit, and repeatedly use the same path to and from favoured feeding areas. These become worn and distinct.

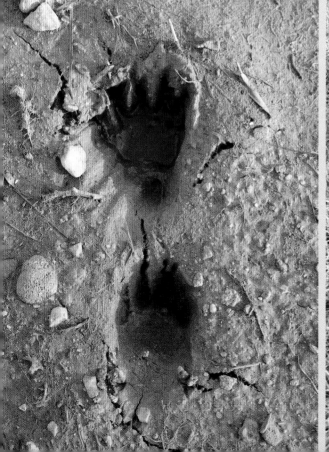

and typically straight route from A to B, with the occasional dig and scuff point where the animal has paused to search for what meagre food resources may be available. On very deep, soft snow, a badger leaves a depression made by its low-slung body between prints.

In addition to individual prints, badgers create well-worn tracks or paths around their territory. These are best defined in the immediate vicinity of a sett (see below) but are also clear where the badgers regularly visit certain fields to forage. Tracks through hedgerows, long grass and even short turf all become worn, leaving either shorter vegetation or totally bare ground. Where badgers trot regularly along shorter sward the effect of their pounding feet alters the vegetation. A line of short-cropped clover, buttercup and a few other hardy plants is often all that grows well along these turf tracks.

FAECES *Dung*

Badgers are almost unique among European wild mammals in their habit of digging pits into which they deposit their dung (see Wildcat page 78). I have never seen a badger, other than one in captivity, leave dung randomly in its transit around the territory. Faecal matter is always deposited in dung pits. These pits serve a very important role as communal scent centres and territory perimeter markers, and tend to be concentrated around natural or man-made boundaries, or close to a sett. Typical locations are field borders (usually tucked up tight against or under a mature hedge), along the base of drystone walls, or by a ditch. If near a sett, dung pits are usually a few metres from the nearest entrance hole alongside a well-worn path.

When a badger's primary food source is earthworms, dung within the pit often looks like nothing more than wet soil (which, in fact, is precisely what it is). Badgers have very catholic tastes, however, and dung colour and form can be enormously variable, with berry seeds, hair, bone fragments or nut remains in the mix. Because several animals from a badger clan use the dung pits communally, you frequently find several different textures and colours of fresh dung in the same shallow pit. At focal points along territory boundaries it is common to find several pits dug in close

Dung is deposited in a shallow pit dug by the badger and used by several members of the same clan. Dung pits are used as territorial marker posts and tend to be clustered along boundaries, such as fence lines and hedges.

proximity to each other, with dung of varying age in each. The remarkable fidelity of clan members to communal dung pits has led research scientists to develop a population study technique whereby food (often peanut butter) is laced with small coloured plastic pellets which travel through the animal's gut and into its faeces. Territory size, boundaries and overlap can be extrapolated by monitoring the coloured pellets in each dung pit. If you happen across a study area you may well encounter these pellets (often orange, blue or green) mixed in the dung within the pits.

Badgers often urinate at the same time as they deposit dung. They also have scent glands near the anus, which they use to mark the ground (and each other). The scent is easily detected by the human nose and is reminiscent of the yeast spread Marmite. I rather like it, but, like Marmite, it's not to everyone's taste!

FEEDING SIGNS

Badgers rarely leave any obvious remains of a meal, but they do leave distinctive signs that they have been foraging. This is almost always some evidence of digging to reach worms or other invertebrates, though their omnivorous diet can lead them to forage on wild and farmed vegetable matter.

Most 'worm digs' are shallow scrapes or snuff holes in grass where the worm has been lying on the surface of the ground. Larger digs are created to access rabbit kits in breeding stops, bumble bee nests and mouse and vole nests. In suitable soil, the badger's distinctive parallel claw marks may be visible in places around the dig.

Badgers are enormously strong for their size and have powerful forequarters and neck muscles. A foraging animal may haul quite large logs and rocks aside in order to reach a tasty grub.

Badgers are one of the few British wild animals capable of breaking through the prickly defences of a hedgehog and, while hedgehogs are ignored as a food item for the most part, there are accounts of badgers killing and eating them. The technique described by observers suggests that the badger manoeuvres the rolled-up hedgehog on to its back, then uses its powerful forefeet and long claws to prise open the animal before finishing the job with its muzzle and

Feeding scrapes vary in size depending on the meal being sought. Many beetle grubs and earthworms are caught as the badger scrapes the topsoil and vegetation away. Such scrapes are usually fairly broad and flat.

strong jaws. Everything apart from the prickly skin on the hedgehog's back is eaten, leaving the rather grim remains of a spiny cape to tell the tale.

While I have found hedgehog skins that were almost certainly the result of badger predation, they have been very few and far between, and during the many thousands of hours I have spent watching badgers foraging by night, I have never witnessed one killing a hedgehog. I have, however, often watched both species feeding side by side on a plentiful food source, such as scraps left out in a back garden by friendly humans, and I have also seen badgers sniff, but otherwise ignore, hedgehogs on their nightly wanderings in rural areas.

While there is no doubt that badgers can, and occasionally do, eat hedgehogs, it is a mistake to attribute the decline in hedgehog numbers in England to badgers. Indeed in the areas where hedgehog numbers have declined most rapidly, badgers are rare or absent. The real causes of falling hedgehog numbers are complex, linked to changes in land use, competition for food items, pesticide use and, to a far lesser extent, predation.

Badgers sometimes raid fields of maize (sweetcorn) and can leave areas flattened with the cobs chewed off. The husks with the kernels removed may be found some distance from the field from which they were pilfered.

Ground-nesting birds are also targeted by badgers and they eat both the eggs and young. Eggshells tend to be left fully shattered in the nest or very close by.

Though badgers could hardly be described as nimble, they are surprisingly good climbers. They can scale reasonably large trees with vertical trunks if the incentive to do so is strong enough, leaving claw and scuff marks on soft bark or algae-covered trunks. Similar parallel claw marks may be found on wooden bridges or decking where badgers slip and slide on wet algae.

HAIR

Badger hair is unique among European mammals in that it is flattened dorsally. If you hold a guard hair between your finger and thumb and try to roll it gently, it either won't move, or else will 'snap' from one flattened side to the

Badgers are partial to the larvae of wasps and bees, many of which nest in the ground. The badger's powerful digging ability allows it to excavate these nests, leaving the insect communities exposed and destroyed. Badgers seem immune to their stings.

Badger hair is frequently found snagged on the lower strands of barbed wire and other wire fences. Its colouration and form are distinctive. Check for hair on fences with well-worn tracks passing beneath them.

other. It is likely that this adaptation helps the badger to move easily through its underground sett and to shed accumulated earth from its pelt.

Hair may be found on the lowest strand of a barbed wire fence, where the animals push beneath the wire, around the sett where grooming has taken place, or in discarded bedding. While badgers appear generally grey at a distance, each guard hair is in fact largely pale cream or white along two-thirds of its length from its base, with a dark blackish band near the tip, terminating in a pale tip. Other body and face hair (which may be white or black) rarely snags on obstacles and so is unlikely to be found.

NOTE: Badger hair has been (and still is) used to make shaving brushes. Most, if not all the badgers killed for this purpose come from the wild in China. Think again before you consider buying a badger hair shaving brush!

HOME

The badger is the quintessential nocturnal creature, foraging under the cover of darkness and spending the day below ground in purpose-dug retreats known as setts. The scale and form of these earthworks depends on a number of factors: the substrate, the size of the clan and the age of the sett. The largest, most obvious setts are usually dug into gently sloping land with easily worked ground, such as sandy or chalky soil, and are often in woodland or on the edge of an established hedgerow. These 'fortresses' are the communities' HQ, and are occupied by well-established, medium-to-large clans of more than six animals. They may have been used by many generations, spanning back decades or even hundreds of years. They have many entrances accessing an unseen labyrinth of hundreds of metres of tunnels and chambers.

Within the territory of a badger clan, there will be smaller annexes or outlying setts and these are used by the animals as places to stop and take a nap, perhaps somewhere to rest to avoid the bustle of a new litter of cubs, or simply a spot close to a summer food source. They are also used as bolt holes – somewhere for the badgers to run to in the face of danger. Nowadays that danger comes largely from people

and their dogs, but until recently in the UK badgers have had to avoid larger predators like wolves and bears, and this is still the case in some parts of their European range.

Badger sett entrances are a minimum of 30cm across, but many of the older, better-established setts have entrances so large that a grown man could wriggle a long way down them. No one should do this, though, as in the UK badgers and their setts are protected by law from disturbance.

Spoil heaps (excavated material) in front of a sett entrance can be vast, often creating flat terraces on otherwise sloping ground. On rocky ground, however, the spoil may be negligible or virtually absent if the badgers are using existing gaps between larger boulders as their retreat.

The key feature that identifies a hole in the ground as belonging to a badger is bedding. Badgers spend up to 70 per cent of their lives in their underground homes and, as they are fastidious creatures, they keep them comfortable and clean. Fresh bedding, in the form of dry grass, leaves or

[ABOVE LEFT] Setts may be no more than a hole between rocks, and outlying setts are often unobtrusive. Main setts may be vast earthworks that have been established by communities of badgers over generations.

[TOP RIGHT] Well-used sett entrances are worn smooth by the repeated passing of badger feet and fur. Some may have dung pits very close by.

[ABOVE] Vegetation for bedding is collected from adjacent fields and woods and brought back to the sett. The badger shuffles backwards with the bedding tucked between its forefeet and held under its chin. You may spot dropped or abandoned bedding rolls just outside the sett entrances.

even fresh torn grass, nettles and other vegetation is gathered by many members of the clan and brought back to the sett. Old bedding is discarded and spread outside the entrance. A careful check of active sett entrances will almost invariably reveal the remains of bedding, often with the odd badger hair mixed in, littering the ground here and there. An active sett is also revealed by the tracks that lead to and from it. Badgers are certainly creatures of habit and on their way to and from foraging grounds they use the same paths, night after night, year after year. As these paths converge on a sett they are frequently void of any vegetation as a result of the repeated trampling of badger feet, and so are a great guide to the observer.

Other clues that identify a badger sett include the scent, claw marks in soil, and even the odd badger skull. A dying badger usually retreats to its underground home and old skulls are frequently tossed up above ground when the residents do a bit of spring cleaning.

HOW TO WATCH

Badger watching was a staple pastime of my youth – not just for me but for a generation of kids with access to the countryside. Indeed, badger watching beats the back row of the movies when it comes to those early, clumsy courting days! What better way to get to know each other, while minimising embarrassment, than sitting silently very close to each other, staring in the same direction into the gloom, waiting for the magic moment when a snuffling badger nose emerges above ground? The moment is shared, conversation impossible and the intimacy absolute!

With very few exceptions, badgers don't like people. In fact, like many wild animals, they are neophobic, that is to say they are afraid of anything new. The best place to try to watch badgers is at their sett, but this must be done with extreme caution so as not to disturb them in any way. Smell is their primary sense, so attention to wind direction is paramount. This can be challenging in a woodland setting and particularly on sloping ground (where big badger setts are often found). Colder evening air is often drawn downhill at dusk, sometimes shifting a prevailing breeze through 180 degrees. Do your best to ensure your scent cannot reach any part of the sett at any time.

Typically, a badger watch requires making reasonable preparation days ahead, and following some simple but strict guidelines. Once you have identified the sett you wish to watch, assess its suitability. A large sett on the far side of a narrow, steep valley and in open woodland

where the prevailing wind allows you to sit on the opposite side of the valley with a clear view is about as good as it gets. A sett in tightly enclosed woodland or a dense hedge, with flat open ground all around it is probably not worth trying to watch.

Prepare your route into, and – crucially – out of the area. Just because you have finished watching the badgers doesn't mean you can stand up and stomp off without a second thought. Try to arrive, and leave, silently. This can be aided by clearing most of the twigs and dead leaves from the path into and out of your watching position. Find a spot where you can stand, or better still, sit, with your back against a tree or other natural feature to hide your outline (page 15). Wear dull-coloured clothing that does not rustle when you move. Take a small cushion or seat pad to make

[ABOVE LEFT] Badgers often target the breeding stops of rabbits, digging out the immobile young. The resulting sign reveals grass bedding, flecked with the belly hair of the mother rabbit, strewn around the stop entrance.

[ABOVE RIGHT] Badgers leave distinctive claw marks where they clamber on logs.

BADGER SENSES

Sound	Sight	Smell
8	**5**	**10**

BADGER'S YEAR

Mating: any time of year, especially just after giving birth in February/March and again in August/September. Delayed implantation ensures that the development of blastocyst doesn't kick off until December, a suspension of 9 months in some cases

Gestation: 7 weeks

Young: 1–5 (usually 3) born in February/March

Emergence of young: cubs usually show their heads above ground in mid-April; 20 April is a common date for first emergence

the wait as comfortable as possible, and a head torch, ideally with a red bulb or filter, to find your way out of the watching position once it is dark. Plan to arrive at the sett two hours before sunset, having eaten something to minimise tummy rumbles. Make sure you have had enough to drink, but not so much that you will need to take a pee anytime in the next four hours or so. The latter is really important as I once found out to my cost!

You may have decided to throw a few peanuts around the sett in the weeks or days leading up to your watch. This should be the last thing you do before settling down since some badgers, especially youngsters, may have become attuned to the sound of the nuts landing on the soil and will emerge soon after they have been thrown down.

Now get as comfortable as possible, and don't move. Remember to be aware of the wind direction and if it does move around, blowing your scent on to the sett, leave the area quietly. If not, you should be rewarded with one of the most magical moments in wildlife watching as the light fades.

If you own a night-viewing device (page 9) you can extend the session into complete darkness. Otherwise, wait until you can no longer see or hear any movement and slip away as quietly as possible. If you have been watching the badgers with a friend, try to avoid talking about your experiences, however tempting that may be, until you are several hundred metres away from the sett.

I used to watch a group of badgers regularly and I found that there were times when I desperately needed to scratch an itch or cough. Both can be done, but you need to practise your technique. Badgers regularly groom themselves and each other soon after emergence and the sound and rhythm of their scratching is distinctive. Once you have heard this enough times it is possible to replicate it to ease your own discomfort, without spooking the animals you are watching. In fact, younger badgers are especially likely to come trotting over to see who their itchy neighbour is!

Coughing is more tricky, but if there is livestock in the fields near where the badgers are living you could mimic either a cow or a sheep coughing to clear your own throat tickle, without unduly bugging the badgers.

OTTER *Lutra lutra*

SIGN

FOOTPRINTS

Otters leave footprints on sandy beaches, on wet mud alongside rivers, lakes and streams, and sometimes in wet soil in places where they cross land to get from one water body to the next. The overall impression is circular, with five radial, teardrop-shaped toes spread widely away from a compact, kidney-shaped heel pad. On firmer sand or soil, only the tips of the toes may show, but the wide spread of the toes, all pointing away from the heel pad, remains distinctive. Claw marks rarely, if ever, show in a natural print, and the same goes for the webs between the toes.

In snow, an otter's low-slung body leaves a distinct drag line, punctuated by near-circular prints from the feet. On sloping ground, otters regularly toboggan in snow, pulling their legs into their sides and sliding on their belly – again leaving a very distinctive gully with no sign of footprints.

OTHER SIGN

Otters use the same route time and again to get from water to a sprainting point (see Faeces page 50), a holt or to another body of water. These tracks are worn smooth by the animal's broad flat feet and low-slung body and, where they pass through vegetation such as long grass or bushes, they create a near-perfect cylindrical form.

SIZE
Weight: 7–12kg
Length to rump: 65–75cm
Tail length: 40–50cm

Front right print (actual size)

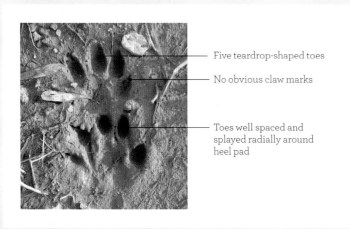

Five teardrop-shaped toes

No obvious claw marks

Toes well spaced and splayed radially around heel pad

Female otters are often accompanied by their young, which may stay with their mother for 14 months or so. By this time male cubs are larger than their mother.

Here and there along an otter trail, you may find places that have been scraped bare of vegetation, often with spraint on the edge. This is where the animal has excitedly scraped with its forefeet before depositing a scent mark.

FAECES *Spraint*

The most distinctive and diagnostic sign that an otter has been about are its droppings, or spraint. This is for a number of reasons. Spraint is usually deposited on a prominent feature, such as a rock in mid-stream, a grassy tussock close to the water's edge or, very typically, beneath a bridge. Otters use their faecal matter in a controlled fashion to ensure there is sufficient spraint to go around the territory, in the much the same manner as a fox or dog urinates to mark its home patch. As a result, some spraints are small, featureless blobs that look more like bird droppings than anything delivered by a large mammal!

Before going into the appearance and location of spraints in more detail I want to describe their most diagnostic feature – their scent. Once you have smelled spraint you

[ABOVE LEFT] Tracks in sand on the coast are ephemeral and, depending on the tide, can be a clue to how recently the otter has passed by.

[ABOVE RIGHT] Close examination of spraint reveals fragments of meals, such as fish bones and scales or crayfish carapace. The scent of spraint is distinctive and easily identified.

[TOP] The otter may gather tufts of vegetation before depositing spraint on the top of the clump. This behaviour is often associated with the actions of a territorial male.

Spraint may be little more than a jelly-like substance containing little or no food fragments [ABOVE CENTRE], or more solid and substantial with bone, scale and shell remains [ABOVE]. All bear a distinctive, sweet scent.

are unlikely to forget it, and not because it is revolting. In fact, in my opinion and that of many others, it is really rather pleasant. The closest common scent I have encountered that resembles spraint is European ivy in full late summer bloom. This shares the sweet, musky, heavy odour of the otter's scent mark, but lacks the fishy overtones. Add a hint of sardine to the scent of ivy flowers, and there you have it!

Sprainting locations vary from habitat to habitat. Otters living along the coast and tidal waters deposit small amounts on rocks that may be covered by the tide, but appear to save their more substantial deposits for features that are less ephemeral. These are often tussocks of grass close to a point where the animals leave or enter the water, on substantial rocks, on bare earth or in the immediate vicinity of a holt (page 53). These otters visit fresh water each day to drink and to wash the salt from their fur, and these watering points will also have a sprainting station nearby. Where otters spraint repeatedly, they alter the chemical balance of the soil, and with it the vegetation. Look out for patches of vivid, dark green grass that has benefited from extra nutrition in an otherwise evenly coloured sward.

Around freshwater lakes, check any prominent features, such as rounded, flat-topped rocks, large fallen trees or areas of bankside vegetation that appear flattened (look out for the narrow, rounded otter trails leading to and from the water here too). On freshwater rivers and streams, check the banks beneath bridges (otters like the security of leaving the water away from the prying eyes of humans), areas of exposed beach or other prominent features such as rocks, tree roots and logs. Otters rarely spraint along trails where they cross a large expanse of land, unless they have a daybed or holt in the vicinity, choosing instead to cover these areas of open ground at a trot without pausing.

Otter spraint has many colours and textures and can be formless or very loosely cylindrical. It is deposited in two main forms – jelly-spraint and solid-spraint. Jelly-spraint appears as nothing more than a small splodge of mucus, often brown or yellow-brown and, when very fresh, this will bear a few air bubbles on its surface. With a little experience it is possible to tell the age of jelly-spraint, based on the prevailing weather conditions, the amount of moisture in

the dropping, the condition of the bubbles on the surface and the pungency of its scent. A wet-looking, bubbly splodge on a rock that is still steaming on a chilly morning is very, very fresh indeed!

Small jelly-spraints contain little or no evidence of what the otter has been eating, but more substantial solid-spraints may contain crab or crayfish shell, fish bones and scales, hair (if the otter has been eating rabbits) or bird feathers. Careful analysis of solid-spraint offers a fount of information about the otter's diet. I have found many more jelly-spraints in coastal environments than I have in freshwater habitats.

In coastal habitats, crabs may make up a significant part of an otter's diet. This young animal is bringing a velvet swimming crab ashore to eat.

FOOD REMAINS

Much of what an otter eats passes through its gut and the remains are only visible in the spraint. Small fish, like butterfish and small eels, are eaten whole while the otter remains floating on the water's surface. Larger fish are brought ashore and either eaten in their entirety, or, in the case of large eels, lumpsuckers, salmon, trout and large carp, the head, spine and caudal fin may be left. When an otter eats a crab, it removes the upper carapace and may discard

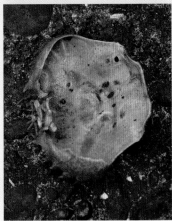

[TOP] An otter may return time and again to a favoured haul-out to feed, leaving the remains of many meals. Here, it's clear that the targeted species has been velvet swimming crabs.

[ABOVE] The carapaces of crabs eaten by an otter often bear distinct holes where they have been penetrated by the animal's canine teeth.

parts of the legs. You may find a near perfect hole or two in a crab carapace, indicating where the otter's upper canine teeth punctured the shell.

Birds such as ducks, coots, moorhens, terns and others, are almost invariably captured on the water, though I did once witness an otter raiding puffin burrows along the top of a high cliff! The otter often consumes the breast meat, leaving the remains relatively intact, with the head, wings and back attached to an open carcass. With rabbits, the otter tends to take the meat from the main body cavity, often leaving the head and legs attached to the skin.

HAIR
Otter hair is incredibly fine and rarely, if ever, found in the wild. As such it is not of value as a field sign.

HOME
Otters rest above ground, in naturally occurring tunnels and cavities and in fashioned burrows, usually enlarged from an existing tunnel made by another animal such as a rabbit. Any place an otter occupies underground is referred to as a holt, while resting places above ground are referred to as lie-ups or couches.

In freshwater environments I have found holts under piles of large logs, in holes through tangled bankside tree roots, in cement culverts and in the gaps between jumbled boulders or derelict man-made structures. Along the coast I have found holts in the jumbled rocks of breakwaters, between natural boulders, in enlarged rabbit burrows and in tunnels adapted in peat banks. In all but those that are used very occasionally, there has been some spraint at or near the entrance hole, often substantial mounds of it that have been deposited over time. Now and then, you may find the remains of vegetation – or, in coastal habitats, seaweed – that has been collected by the otter (using its mouth) for bedding, and which has either been discarded or left half in, half out of an entrance hole. The best-used holts have clear otter runs leading to and from them. Many, but by no means all, are close to the water's edge and, particularly in coastal areas, I have watched many occupied holts that were several hundred metres away from the water's edge. Some have

even been near the crest of large hills! There is often a ditch or small brook close to these inland holts, which the otters use as a highway and a place to wash and drink.

Even a very well-used holt may show little sign of occupancy besides spraint deposits, and nursery holts may lack even these in close proximity to the holt entrance. In peat, repeated visits will have worn the entrance smooth, but in jumbles of rocks it is very hard to tell precisely where the animals may be entering and leaving without direct observation.

HOW TO WATCH

Techniques for observing otters vary according to habitat type: coastal, fresh still water or fresh flowing water. Of the three, coastal otter watching is most successful as a rule, since the body clock of the animals in this habitat is governed by the tide more than the sun, and so they are far more likely to be seen in daylight.

In each of these habitats, certain criteria remain consistent. Wind direction is of paramount importance, since the otter's sense of smell is incredibly acute and it will pick up the scent of a human at several hundred metres in the right conditions. The other senses are far less sharp, though the outline of a human against the skyline will cause alarm in all but the most habituated wild otter.

In a coastal environment, first check the tide tables. A dropping or low tide at, or close to, dawn is perfect.

[ABOVE LEFT] Holts in coastal regions may be in peat hags, and are often extended rabbit burrows. The area outside a well-used holt is worn clear of vegetation and will be peppered with spraint.

[ABOVE RIGHT] Runs to and from holts are narrow and, where they pass through dense vegetation, often form a near-cylindrical tunnel.

Sound	Sight	Smell
8	5	10

High water at dawn is the least desirable. This is because the otters are likely to be at their busiest when the tide is at, or approaching, its lowest point, but nonetheless prefer to move around early in the day before there is a strong likelihood of human activity. On quiet stretches of coastline, otters may be active throughout the day, depending on the tide. An average activity period is usually in the region of two hours, depending on the animal's hunting success (the more successful, the shorter the activity period) and encounters with other otters, which may prolong the action. There are usually two activity bouts in a 24-hour period.

Having decided on a suitable tide, look at the weather forecast for the prevailing wind direction and consult a good map of the area. You are looking for a stretch of suitable coastline habitat that will ensure the wind is blowing your scent inland as you walk the foreshore. Also look for areas of high ground that you can use as initial observation posts. Having picked your coastline and a suitable high point, get out bright and early and settle down to scour the water. A calm day makes it much easier to pick up the form of a surface-swimming otter, which leaves a long 'V' in its wake. Windy days create more chop on the water's surface, making it harder to spot the otter's low swimming profile.

Otters are not alone in creating a 'V' shaped wake, of course. Seals, cormorants, mergansers and many other creatures can cut a similar form and trail through the water, and just to add to the confusion they all dive too! There are key points that separate an otter from everything else. The otter has a very low profile in the water, showing two, if not three 'humps' made by the animal's head, back and tail. Seals usually show only one or two humps – the head and sometimes the back. Birds will, sooner or later, lift their heads and reveal themselves for what they are.

The diving profile of a relaxed otter is distinctive too, as is its surfacing profile. Just before submerging, an otter snatches a breath, lifting its head slightly, then arcs its head and body down in a 'duck dive' and flicks its tail in the air as it disappears. It surfaces head first and pops up like a cork briefly before settling on the surface with its usual low profile. This 'corking' is really eye-catching once you get used to it, and I scour the water's surface with the naked eye

After snowfall, holts may be clearly defined by the runs made by an otter's low-slung body. The animal forms slides as it pushes itself along through the snow.

watching for this very distinctive flash of a surfacing otter, before deploying my binoculars to confirm the sighting.

Once you have spotted your otter at a distance, check its direction of travel, then study the coastline. Keeping the wind direction in mind, look for a promontory or headland that lies in the otter's path, and aim to reach it before the otter does. This can be done carefully at a distance but as you get closer to the water be mindful of your profile (page 15). Once you get to within 100 metres or so, consider only moving when the otter dives, then freezing when it is on the surface – playing a form of grandmother's footsteps! If all goes well, you should reach the promontory before the otter is close and have time to settle in, with the wind taking your scent inland and your outline masked by rocks or another feature.

With luck, the otter will come on to land to scent mark on the same promontory. With more luck, it will bring a large fish to consume on the shore in front of you, and with even more good fortune, it may come ashore for a rest, curling up to sleep in the seaweed or on a rock. You could also stake out a holt or a freshwater drinking point, but given that an otter may use different parts of its home range each day, you might be in for a long wait.

Mobility is key to successful otter watching on the coast. There are exceptions to this approach where otters are very familiar with human activity, such as at ferry ports and breakwaters near human habitation, but even here anything out of the ordinary, such as a human pursuing an otter for a closer look, will be regarded with suspicion and is likely to drive the animal into cover.

On bodies of still freshwater, I have found the 'wait and see' method is most successful. Having established that the area is used by otters by finding their sign, pick a suitable lookout point on the banks of the lake, always keeping your scent blowing away from the water, and wait for the low profile of a swimming otter to come into view. Most lakes and lochs have thick vegetation on the shoreline, so views of the otter on land in these habitats are rare and unpredictable. The only exception to this is if the water freezes, forcing the otters to run across the ice to reach areas of open water. I have had great sightings of otters on English lakes and

OTTER'S YEAR

Mating: no season, though often mid-winter in England, and late spring and early summer in Scotland

Gestation: 62–63 days

Young: 2–3 cubs

Emergence of young: cubs emerge from natal holt at about 7 weeks; first swim at about 3 months

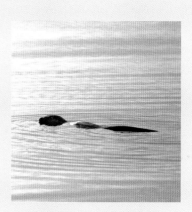

The distinctive 'three humps' of a relaxed otter on the surface of a sea loch. An otter that suspects danger can submerge its body and tail, leaving only its eyes, ears and nose visible.

Otters may be extremely difficult to spot when they are feeding among floating seaweed. Watch for the roll of an otter's back or the flick of its muscular tail as it dives.

Scottish lochs at all times of day, but early morning and late evening have been the most reliable activity periods, as well as through the night, of course, often just after nightfall.

Running fresh water is perhaps the most challenging environment for otter watching. Rivers and streams represent a linear resource for the otters, and they can cover several kilometres of waterway in a single foraging trip. They also tend to move through their territory on a cyclical basis, depending on food resources, and may be in one area for a day or two, another for the next couple of days and so on. Add to this their tendency for nocturnal foraging and you have a recipe for very frustrating otter-watching attempts. There are notable exceptions in rivers where otters have become so familiar with benign human activity that they forage regularly in broad daylight in full view of people – paying little or no attention to human scent or movement, but these are still rare on a national or international scale.

If you have established that otters are using a river or stream through their sign, then staking out likely foraging pools is the best observation technique. Apply all the usual precautions and I recommend the use of night-viewing equipment (page 9) if you are planning a nocturnal vigil.

WEASEL *Mustela nivalis*

SIGN

FOOTPRINTS

Under normal conditions, you are extremely unlikely to find a weasel's footprint. Weasels spend most of their lives scurrying through dense undergrowth or in and out of vole runs and mouse holes, rarely venturing into the open. On the rare occasions when they do – for example, when dashing across a road or track – they almost invariably do so in a bounding gait. If they should happen to make contact with soil that has just the right consistency and level of moisture, they may leave prints. These are tiny, about the same size as a brown rat's or slightly smaller, with five toes on each foot and prominent claw marks.

Weasels do not hibernate, so if there is significant snowfall, you may find tracks where a weasel has come out of the network of vole runs it usually inhabits. These tracks tend to be in clumped pairs as a result of the bounding gait of a running animal but again, unless the snow consistency is perfect, the print is rarely more than a depression.

FAECES *Scat or droppings*

Weasels are very discreet with their droppings and the vast majority are deposited well away from the gaze of humans. Exceptionally, weasels may leave deposits of droppings

SIZE

Male larger than female
Weight: 55–130g
Length to rump: 17–21cm
Tail length: 4cm
Height at shoulder: 3–4cm

**Front left print
(actual size)**   **Rear left print
(actual size)**

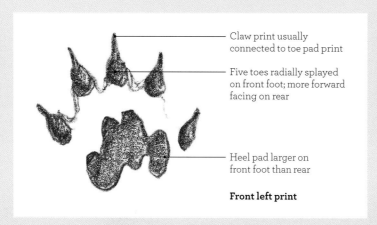

Claw print usually connected to toe pad print

Five toes radially splayed on front foot; more forward facing on rear

Heel pad larger on front foot than rear

Front left print

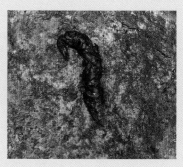

Weasel scat is small – about 1–1.5cm long and 2–3mm thick – and usually dark and twisted. It often contains small mammal hair.

close to the entrance of a regularly used den, such as a hole in a drystone wall or in a hollow log. The droppings tend to be no longer than 1–1.5cm and 2–3mm thick, very narrow and twisted with a black sheen. Small mammal hair may be found within the dropping. The scent is not pleasant, with a heavy acrid musk.

FOOD REMAINS

Weasels target small mammals, largely voles and mice, and take their prey to a secluded spot to devour it. They can tackle animals significantly larger than themselves, from small rabbits to medium-sized birds, and they also raid birds' nests for both chicks and eggs.

To eat an egg, a weasel often breaks it across the widest part by lodging its upper canines in the shell and drawing its lower jaw into the egg. As a result, two tiny holes may be left in the shell from the anchoring upper canines. These are less than a centimetre apart and look as though they have been made with a pin.

The flight feathers and larger body feathers of birds are chewed rather than cleanly bitten or plucked out, and the frayed, chewed quills are a distinctive sign that a small mustelid has made the kill. It is very difficult to distinguish between stoat and weasel kills using this sign alone.

HOME

Weasels do not make a den as such but instead use existing cavities such as holes in stone walls, rocky outcrops and hollow logs. They will also adopt the empty nests of mice, voles and other prey, sometimes leaving the remains of their last meals in and around the nest. In some regions, they compress the hair of dead rodents into a nest lining. Such retreats have no distinctive sign besides the possible deposit of droppings nearby, or prey within.

This blackbird egg has been predated by a weasel. Note the 'M' shape on the upper section of the hole, created by the weasel's canine teeth.

WEASEL SENSES

Sound
6

Sight
6

Smell
3

WEASEL'S YEAR

Mating: March–July

Gestation: 34–37 days

Young: 1 or 2 litters of 4–8 kits per year

Emergence of young: 5–6 weeks

HOW TO WATCH

Weasel watching is a reactive rather than a proactive pursuit. The opportunities you may have to head out specifically to watch a weasel will be limited to having discovered a den in which a female has young kits, or having encountered a weasel hunting in a more open habitat. You can then go to the spot in the hope of another sighting. The trouble is that, despite their small size, weasels move around a great deal and cover large areas. Even a prime hunting site may be visited only once or twice a year, so to see a weasel you really have to trust to luck.

If you do encounter a weasel, it may be bold and inquisitive, sometimes coming quite close to an observer to get a better look. This behaviour can be encouraged by mimicking a vole squeaking (page 186).

Small birds, especially wrens and dunnocks, mob weasels if they spot them and the enraged alarm calls of these and other birds may draw your attention. In such a circumstance, watch the gaze of the birds giving the alarm for a clue as to the whereabouts of the little predator.

STOAT *Mustela erminea*

SIGN

FOOTPRINTS

Like weasels, stoats tend to stick to thick cover, though since they are larger and often target rabbit prey, stoats travel over open ground more frequently than their diminutive cousins. Nonetheless, tracks are few and far between. On wet mud or snow, the five-toed prints show clear claw marks, with toes well splayed around the hind pad.

FAECES *Scat or droppings*

Each dropping is elongated, thin and twisted, often black, with small mammal hair visible in the tapering end. It measures about 3cm long and 5mm wide. The scent is a heavy, sour musk.

FOOD REMAINS

Stoats are adaptable predators and tackle anything up to the size of a mature rabbit. Most prey is killed with a single bite to the back of the head or neck, though larger prey may require a more concerted effort to despatch.

Even large kills are carried or dragged off to a secluded place to eat. A rabbit carcass stuck in a cavity of a stone wall is almost certainly the work of a stoat that has misjudged the size of its prey when trying to stash it. Like weasels, stoats chew the flight and larger feathers from their avian prey,

SIZE
Male about 10 per cent larger than female
Weight: 140–440g
Length to rump: 24–31cm
Tail length: about 10cm
Height at shoulder: 5–6cm

Front right print (actual size)

Clear claw marks

Five, long, forward-facing toes

Tiny heel pad may leave little or no mark

Stoat scat is typical of a mustelid – twisted, dark and with tapered ends. Clusters may be found at latrine points.

leaving frayed quill ends. They devour smaller prey in its entirety, but discard larger bones and fur. With rabbit prey, the legs, head and skin may be left in a twisted cape after the stoat has finished feeding. If a stoat is disturbed at a rabbit kill before it has had time to eat much, the carcass will reveal the stoat's killing method of biting repeatedly at the back of the prey's head and neck. This is also often the point at which the stoat will start feeding.

While stoats can easily chase and kill rabbits within their burrow system, they also make flat-out pursuits above ground. A stoat will charge relentlessly after a targeted animal until it can catch up with it, mount its back and deliver a bite to the back of the neck. Such kills rarely leave many signs besides a few tufts of rabbit hair at the kill site, though the rabbit under attack will scream and draw the observer's attention.

Birds' nests and eggs are targeted too. You will see bite traces on eggshells, the two upper canines leaving clear puncture holes a little over 1cm apart.

Stoats are good climbers and swimmers (though they do not readily dive underwater) and I have watched a stoat chase a bank vole into a river and catch it halfway across while still swimming. In areas where water voles are common they are a preferred prey of stoats.

HOME
Holes in walls, cavities under buildings, hollow logs and log piles may be adopted by stoats as den sites. No bedding is collected, though the hair of past kills may line a nest if exposed. Middens of scat may be left within a metre or so of a den entrance.

WINTER COAT
Stoats do not hibernate, and in cold northern climates they develop a white winter coat, known as ermine.

STOAT'S YEAR
Mating: April–June; delayed implantation; full development usually starts the following March

Active gestation: 4 weeks

Young: 1 litter of 6–12 kits

Emergence of young: June/July at about 7–8 weeks old

Sound
6

Sight
6

Smell
3

HOW TO WATCH

Unlike weasels, stoats can be reasonably visible when hunting rabbits and when denning. If you find a den site, take care not to disturb the inhabitants; a female will move young kits if she feels they may be under threat. Stoats may be bold or nervous, depending on their experiences of humans. Many regard us as their arch enemies and so are quite understandably very timid; others may run to within a metre or so of the observer.

A favoured hunting territory, such as a rabbit warren, is a great place to stoat watch. Patient stake-outs, using reasonable cover, may pay dividends and a simple field hide (page 24) will help break up an observer's outline. While stoats have a good sense of smell, they do not appear to react negatively to human scent unless very close by, so wind direction is of low concern.

Most sightings of stoats are serendipitous, when the animal dashes across a track or road in front of the observer. Also, you could try mimicking a vole squeaking (page 186). They often respond well and may run to within a couple of metres of you.

POLECAT *Mustela putorius*

SIGN

FOOTPRINTS

Polecats move through an often heavily vegetated environment in a way that makes tracks hard to come by. When polecats do cross soft muddy ground, or snow, their prints are easy to confuse with those of a mink, which may be of a similar size (gender and age result in a wide range of sizes).

Polecat tracks are less splayed than those of mink, especially the forefeet. The toes are more forward facing and more likely to display claw marks, which may be straight or crooked and start about 6mm from the tip of the toe pad. If mink claws show in a print they tend to be closer to the toe pad.

Also like mink, five toes may show on fore or hind footprints on very soft ground, but in most conditions only four toes show. Heel pads may appear kidney shaped or as three closely grouped plantar pads.

FAECES *Scat or droppings*

Droppings are elongated, thin and twisted, often black, with small mammal hair visible in the tapering ends. They measure 6–7cm long and about 7mm wide and the scent is a heavy, sour musk.

SIZE

Weight: M 1.2kg; F 700g
Length to rump: M 41cm; F 35cm
Length of tail: M 15cm F 12cm

Rear left print (actual size)

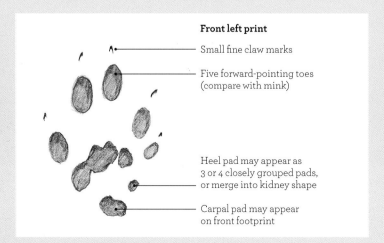

Front left print

— Small fine claw marks

— Five forward-pointing toes
(compare with mink)

— Heel pad may appear as
3 or 4 closely grouped pads,
or merge into kidney shape

— Carpal pad may appear
on front footprint

Although polecats are largely nocturnal, a patient vigil in a suitable habitat, especially in midsummer, may result in views.

FOOD REMAINS

Polecats take a broad range of prey, predominantly mammals such as rabbits, voles and mice. Seasonally they also prey on frogs and toads as well as birds (eggs, chicks and occasionally adults).

Remains of mammal prey may have inverted skin attached to the skeleton (similar to stoat kills) and there may be killing wounds at the base of the neck or skull.

When frogs and toads are available in breeding ponds, polecats may take large numbers and stash them away. They may leave toad heads intact (probably to avoid eating the poison glands), though puncture wounds in the cranium will indicate where the polecat's canines have delivered a killing bite. Frogs may be stashed in a suitable cache and may have their heads bitten to immobilise them, but are otherwise left intact (and sometimes still alive) as a fresh larder.

POLECAT'S YEAR

Mating: March–early May

Gestation: 42 days

Young born: 1 litter of 5–10 young born May–July

Emergence of young: from 6 weeks old

Compared to their domesticated form (known as ferrets or polecat ferrets), polecats are more slender and have an alert attitude. The distinctive 'bandit' mask varies in intensity of colour and coverage of the face.

POLECAT SENSES

Sound	Sight	Smell
7	**6**	**7**

HOME

Polecats use any existing burrow or hole, especially the burrows of rabbits, the original owners of which they will eat! They may occupy several den sites over a home range and there will be little regular activity in any other than natal dens. There may be large scat middens near well-used den sites and prey remains may litter the ground outside natal dens.

HOW TO WATCH

This is a tough animal to watch in the wild. Truly wild, full-blood polecats are nervous animals and in many parts of their range they are almost exclusively nocturnal.

In midsummer, I have had some success watching polecats, by staking out large rabbit warren systems and spotting the predators as they arrived at dusk or hunted at dawn. I deployed the standard 'sit and wait' method with minimal camouflage, but was mindful of wind direction, ensuring my scent was not blowing across the warren. Elsewhere, watching from a hide, I've seen a polecat family coming to drink at a small pond, and close to my home in Somerset I found, quite by chance, a breeding den, with small but mobile kits playing around the exterior.

Polecats can and do breed with escaped domestic ferrets and there are many places in the UK and elsewhere where polecat-ferrets live wild. These animals tend to be larger, often with variable colouring, and with a more relaxed demeanour and attitude than pure polecats. Some have very similar markings, but if the animal is easy to watch, the chances are it's not a pure polecat.

AMERICAN MINK *Neovison vison*

SIGN

FOOTPRINTS

Due to their habit of following waterways, mink may leave footprints in damp, bankside mud and sandbars. These prints reveal well-splayed toes which have a star-like appearance and are separated from the heel pad by a significant gap. On very soft ground five toes on both forefeet and hind feet may show, but more often prints reveal four toes on the forefoot and five on the hind. Claws show up well and usually appear to be joined to the toe pad, creating a teardrop shape.

FAECES *Scat or droppings*

Mink leave their scat on prominent points such as rocks on a riverbank or under bridges. They vary in colour and texture, depending on the diet, but usually appear blackish and may be twisted and full of mammal hair, or looser when containing fish or crustacea remains. Though scat may superficially resemble an otter spraint in colour, form and location, one sniff sets them apart – mink scat is foul smelling compared to otter spraint (page 50) and has an acrid, burnt rubber scent.

SIZE

Male larger than female
Weight: 700g–1kg
Length to rump: 36–40cm
Tail length: 13–15cm

Front right print (actual size) in moderately dry soil

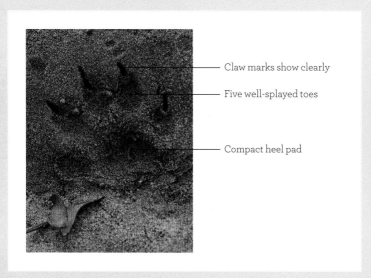

Claw marks show clearly

Five well-splayed toes

Compact heel pad

Mink scat is typically long and twisted, though it may be loose in form depending on the diet. It may contain anything from small mammal hair to fish and bird remains.

Mink are often encountered near water, in which they swim and dive well.

FOOD REMAINS

Mink tackle almost anything they can overpower, up to large birds like ducks and herons as well as mammals the size of adult rabbits. They dive well and they will swim to catch prey in water, including eels, crayfish and larger, free-swimming fish.

Prey remains reveal the tell-tale signs of a mustelid at work, including chewed feather quills and neat, relatively small holes in the skin of the prey made to access muscle tissue within. On fish, there may be discreet tooth marks in the flesh, with the large fins and often the head left intact. (Otters tend to eat the entire fish except when dealing with the very largest species like carp and pike, when they will leave the head and tail, and occasionally the saddle.)

Mink can have an enormously negative impact on water vole populations, since they are able to follow these rodents into their aquatic habitat (a water vole's usual escape strategy) and dive below the surface in hot pursuit. As a result, American mink have been largely responsible for wiping out water vole populations in much of the UK. The general biodiversity of British waterways undoubtedly suffers with a high American mink population.

American mink first colonised the UK in the 1920s as escapees from fur farms. With no similar predator filling their niche, and otter populations at an all time low, mink began to flourish and spread.

Mink often step with their rear foot in the print left by their front foot. Here the footprints of water voles can be seen in the mud around the marks left by the mink, their arch enemy.

We now have direct evidence that where otter populations are thriving, mink numbers are reduced and those that co-exist are subordinate to otters in all hunting situations. Mink are an invasive, non-native species in the UK and have had significant impact on the populations of some species of native wildlife, especially water voles and some birds, such as moorhens. Unless complete eradication of mink in an area is achieved, it may be preferable to allow territorial animals to remain. These have the effect of excluding nomadic mink searching for a territory of their own, which might otherwise congregate in higher numbers than a territory can support. While it is undoubtedly a great shame that American mink found their way into the wilds of Europe, more work has to be done to decide the best course of action to minimise their impact on native fauna.

The European mink is a different species and does not occur in the UK. It is critically endangered and occurs in small numbers in Eastern Europe, Spain and France.

HOME
I have found mink breeding dens in culverts close to waterways, log piles and, on the coast, in cavities in jumbles of rocks. All these have been discovered by serendipity (seeing a mink poke its head out of a hole), though on close inspection, some scat was present within a few metres of each of these sites. Where the entrance to the den includes soil and vegetation, narrow runs and subtle scrapings appear as a result of the repeated traffic of the animals.

HOW TO WATCH
When mink were still escaping from fur farms in the UK (at the industry's peak there were more than 400 fur farms breeding mink to supply the fashion business, not to mention the unofficial breeders), many of the animals encountered were incredibly tolerant of humans. The last farm closed in the late 1990s and since then the feral population has grown progressively wary of humans. Despite having been bred in a variety of fur colours, from near-white through silver-grey to black, the wild population in Europe has now almost entirely reverted to the natural dark chocolate-brown fur of the native population in the Americas.

MINK SENSES

Sound	Sight	Smell
6	6	6

AMERICAN MINK'S YEAR
Mating: February/March

Gestation: variable, with potential to delay implantation; 36–76 days

Young: 1 litter of 4–6 young (up to 17 in captivity) born in May/June

Emergence of young: usually in July/August at 5–6 weeks

Mink are enormously adaptable and versatile. They are active by night and day, and equally at home on land, in fresh water or along the coastline.

Apart from at a breeding den, the likelihood of seeing a mink in the wild almost certainly depends on a chance encounter. The males range over a huge area and can cover many kilometres of waterways, hedgerows and fields. While the females have much smaller territories, they keep a very low profile and are often nocturnal. Mink are equally at home hunting by night or day. In areas where otters are most active by night in the same territory as a mink, there is some evidence to suggest that the mink will adopt a diurnal cycle to avoid conflict. That said, there is lots of evidence showing mink and otter active within a few metres of each other by both day and night.

As mink are generalist hunters, they can be encountered in almost any habitat, but you are most likely to see one in fresh water and coastal territories. This is partly due to their preference for using these areas for hunting, and also because a mink on or near water is much more visible than one hunting in thick vegetation.

I have seen a mink catching eels within a few metres of where I was standing and bringing them to the bank near my feet to feed, apparently indifferent to my presence. This was in the 1970s and the animal was almost certainly one that had not long been out of a fur farm.

A female at the den can be very wary, and may react negatively to human scent. Standard precautions of concealment and awareness of wind direction should be taken.

PINE MARTEN *Martes martes*

SIGN

FOOTPRINTS

You may find marten prints in damp mud that is just the right consistency, but generally these secretive creatures keep to thick ground cover or trees, making the likelihood of encountering their tracks very slim during the summer.

In winter and during periods of snow cover, the reverse is true, since martens do not hibernate and must range far and wide in search of a meal. Tracks in soft snow are almost always paired, and separated by the bounding jumps made by the marten as it covers the ground. These pairs usually have the forefoot track partially covered by the hind foot, which very nearly replaces the forefoot impression in the snow. In harder snow, the marten may adopt a trotting or walking gait and these tracks are likely to show more distinct separation between forefeet and hind feet. The front foot of a pine marten has a small but well-defined carpal pad which may show up in firm snow or mud and is diagnostic.

In winter, the pine marten's feet become so thickly furred that pad marks may become quite indistinct and impressions in the snow may look much larger than the animal's size would suggest. Beech martens do not occur

SIZE

Male slightly larger than female
Weight: 900g–2.2kg
Length to rump: 46–54cm
Tail length: 18–27cm
Height at shoulder: 15–20cm

Rear print (actual size)

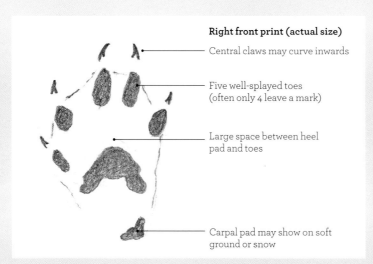

Right front print (actual size)

Central claws may curve inwards

Five well-splayed toes
(often only 4 leave a mark)

Large space between heel
pad and toes

Carpal pad may show on soft
ground or snow

Martens typically move in a bounding gait, leaving paired prints in snow. Rear footprints often overlap those made by the front feet.

Pine marten scat is usually dark and twisted, and deposited on a prominent feature, such as a grass tuft or rock.

in the British Isles, and where the two species' ranges overlap on the European continent, their tracks are virtually indistinguishable.

FAECES *Scat or droppings*

Pine martens use their droppings as smelly calling cards (in much the same way as otters and foxes do). They are typically thin, long and evenly rod shaped, though often curled into twists and kinks (a classic pine marten scat forms a roughly heart-shaped curl). Depending on the animal's diet, the scat may contain small mammal hair, feathers, insect remains and/or traces of wild fruits, and they are usually very dark brown or black. They are often left in prominent places, such as on top of stones by woodland rides or on wide fence posts and fallen logs. A marten returns to the same scat point repeatedly to top up its scented border marker. The scat has a faintly musky scent, not foul to the nose, nor especially sweet. Where a marten creates a latrine, which they may do close to a den or resting hollow, quantities of scat and urine may build up. The scent is unpleasant to the human nose.

FOOD REMAINS

Pine martens are generalist omnivores, although strictly speaking they are carnivores. They eat a lot of fruit when it's available and can adapt their diet to abundant food sources. In the autumn they are partial to ripening berries and at any time of year can be tempted to feed on jam or peanut butter (neither of which is good for them). They are beautifully adapted for arboreal hunting and are a major predator of squirrels, both red and grey. Indeed, there is strong evidence to suggest that where red and grey squirrels live side by side, pine martens have greater success when hunting the non-native grey. This may be due to the grey squirrel's larger size, making it harder for it to escape to the thinnest branches of a tree that will not support the weight of a hunting marten. The lighter red squirrel can utilise this advantage.

A great deal of hunting is conducted at ground level, targeting voles and other small mammals, as well as invertebrates and berries. With such broad tastes, there is little a pine marten does not have access to, with the exception of aquatic animals and plants.

Martens take birds' eggs and eat them in the tree or on the ground. They discard the shells, which may be found on the ground beneath the point where the marten has fed. They may eat ground-nesting birds' eggs in the nest itself, but more often carry them away, one by one, to consume in a quiet spot. Martens usually bite an egg across its width, creating a neat rectangular cavity with their lower jaw, before lapping up the contents (compare to fox, stoat, weasel and badger).

Small birds and nestlings may be eaten whole, but the large feathers of bigger bird species are chewed from the wing; body feathers are usually plucked. Voles and other small mammals are usually eaten in their entirety, though the gut and some internal organs may be discarded.

HOME

Holes in trees, hollow logs and tangled roots are favoured den sites. Cairns and gaps in rocky outcrops are often used too. Pine martens will sometimes shelter in outbuildings, especially if they are able to access the roof space. A friend who lives on the west coast of Scotland, found a marten that used a large polystyrene box stored in the roof of an outhouse as its sleeping quarters. Large nest boxes (the type usually put up for owls or tree-nesting ducks) are readily deployed, and specially designed marten boxes are often occupied. Martens leave little sign that they are using a den site, other than the occasional scat and urine middens nearby, and perhaps slight smear marks at the entrance to the den. They do not gather bedding but make use of any wood chip or other material they find within a void. Old squirrel drey sites in tree hollows or nest boxes are a favourite choice.

HOW TO WATCH

Where pine martens are used to visiting human settlements for food (often the food put out for birds on a bird table) they can be remarkably confiding and predictable. I have enjoyed many wonderful views of these charming creatures as they visit well-stocked feeding stations by night throughout the year and at dusk during the summer months. In areas where they do not regularly encounter the scent, sight and sound of benign humans, martens are generally timid and difficult to

PINE MARTEN'S YEAR

Mating: mid to late summer, often July

Gestation: delayed implantation of 5.5–6.5 months; post-implantation gestation 30 days

Young born: 1–4 young born March/April

Emergence of young: June/July

PINE MARTEN SENSES

Sound	Sight	Smell
10	8	6

The spot marks and borders of the marten's pale bib are unique to each animal and can be used by observers to distinguish individuals in a population.

observe. This is largely because they still suffer from direct human persecution, despite being rare in the British Isles. They are restricted to the wilder parts of Scotland and Ireland, with a handful still breeding in North Wales and northern England. Much of their activity occurs during the hours of darkness, and daylight encounters tend to be only at dusk and dawn. The exception to this is when young kits start to venture beyond the natal den and they may come out in broad daylight to stretch their legs and play.

Besides watching martens coming to feeding stations and the odd chance encounter in old oak forests on the west coast of Scotland, I have seen very few in the wild. I watched one animal hunting over an area of clear felled forest in Scotland for several nights in a row, which allowed me to pick a position and wait for its arrival at dusk. It spent a great deal of time stopping, watching and listening for its prey, occasionally standing high on its back legs on a tree stump to get a panoramic view of its surroundings

Throughout this activity, the marten depended largely on its superb hearing to locate its prey, which it eventually did, catching a vole by leaping into the air and coming down hard on the spot where the vole was moving through the grass. As I watched, I remained downwind, with my back to a tree stump, and motionless. At no point was I detected.

WILDCAT *Felis silvestris*

SIGN

FOOTPRINTS

The print of a wildcat is very like that of a large domestic cat, with which this species regularly hybridises. The four, forward-facing toes all lie before the kidney-shaped heel pad which has three lobes, creating a circular-looking track. There are no claw marks, as the claws are retracted during normal walking gait. True wildcats are often larger than the majority of domestic cats, and the print tends to be longer than it is wide, a trait which is usually reversed in domestic cats. Given the variability of the latter in size (from the giant Maine Coon to tiny miniature breeds) it is very hard to say with certainty that you have found the footprint of a pure blood wildcat.

FAECES *Scat or droppings*

As you might expect, wildcat scat looks very like the droppings of a feral cat. These tend to be cylindrical, with twists and tapered ends and are often full of small mammal hair or feather remains. A wildcat may dig pits and deposit droppings in them, though more commonly it scrapes the ground or vegetation a little before depositing its scat in an open site. The scent is musky and catlike; not pleasant to my nose!

SIZE

Weight: M 3.5–7.1kg; F 2.5–5.6kg
Length to rump: M 56cm; F 54cm
Tail length: about 30cm
Height at shoulder: about 35cm

Front left print (actual size)

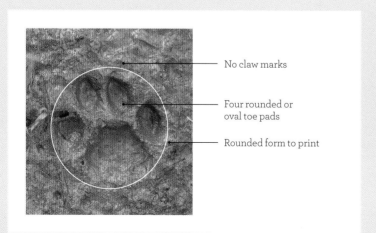

No claw marks

Four rounded or oval toe pads

Rounded form to print

FOOD REMAINS

This species ranges widely in hunting forays. Females (known as pusses) carry prey back to dependent young, but lots of kills are eaten where they are made if the cat is undisturbed. Some kills are taken into trees to be eaten, and the remains of both birds and mammals may be found in low branches. Feathers of larger birds are scissored from the wings with the carnassial teeth, leaving clean cuts at the quill base. Otherwise, the remains of medium-sized mammals, such as rabbits, hares and deer fawns, as well as larger birds, have a very similar appearance to those from kills made by foxes. Muscle tissue has usually been chewed from leg and wing bones, and hair and some skin pulled back and left still attached to the limbs.

HAIR

Wildcat scat is often deposited on vegetation or in a shallow scrape.

I have never come across wildcat hair in the wild. It is fine and variable in colour but unlikely to provide reliable evidence of the species' presence, given its similarity to that of a domestic tabby cat.

HOME

This is a hunter of remote forests and open country. Of the wildcats I have watched (and they have been few and far between), most were fleeting glimpses of animals moving through rough heather and boulder country in the west Scottish Highlands. I once had more protracted views of a hunting female which was regularly visiting open rough grassland in an area of new forestry plantation in the central Highlands. This cat often used the same point of entry and exit to the hunting grounds from an area of thick trees, where I was confident she had hidden young kittens. From time to time, she would jump up to the top of a fence post to scan the area before dropping down to the ground to hunt. After making a kill, often a vole but sometimes an immature rabbit, she would cautiously return to her young, often looking back over her shoulder. As she approached the forest edge she appeared to be calling, but she was too far away for me to hear her.

WILDCAT'S YEAR

Mating: February–April

Gestation: 66 days

Young born: 3–4 kittens, usually in May

Emergence of young: first come out of the den at 4–5 weeks

Once widespread all over the UK, wildcats are now extremely rare and occur only in the wilder parts of Scotland.

WILDCAT SENSES

Sound
10

Sight
10

Smell
8

Breeding dens may be in rocky outcrops, in heather clumps or under large logs. Very little sign betrays their presence, though as the kittens mature, kill remains may litter the ground nearby and there may be signs of trampling in surrounding vegetation. The light-footed nature of this species means that the trampling is unlikely to be as pronounced as that seen around the breeding earth of a fox.

OTHER SIGN

Scratch marks on trees (often low down in the bark of oak and Scots pine) may be used by wildcats as marking posts. They leave a scent from glands between the toes which is not detectable to the human nose. Scratch marks higher up the tree may be made by a climbing cat, but they are very subtle indeed.

HOW TO WATCH

True full-blood wildcats don't like humans. The extreme rarity of this animal in Britain is due in large part to past persecution by fur trappers and by gamekeepers protecting grouse moors and other shooting interests. You can forgive the cats for not wanting to rub shoulders with us!

Wildcats are largely nocturnal and the few that are left keep to remote country where they are unlikely to encounter humans. Females tending dependent young may hunt at dusk and dawn and so may be watched without the aid of specialist night-viewing equipment.

Fantastic eyesight, uncanny hearing ability and a pretty good sense of smell make the wildcat a challenging animal to watch at close quarters. All the same methods one would use to watch a wild rural fox apply (page 36), with perhaps even greater emphasis on camouflage.

RED DEER *Cervus elaphus*

SIGN

FOOTPRINTS

In common with all even-toed ungulates, red deer tracks reveal two roughly symmetrical 'toes' (cloven hooves). Red deer are the biggest deer species in Britain and the large size of their hoof prints (see opposite) is the best clue to the species that produced them. There is some overlap, though, between the prints of a small red deer hind or a half-grown calf and those of a large sika stag or fallow deer buck. Red deer prints look fatter and are generally more oval shaped and rounded than those of other deer species likely to be found in Britain or Europe. Prints made by hinds are smaller and more delicate than those made by stags.

OTHER SIGN

Key red deer sign, besides their footprints, are wallows, fraying stocks (see opposite) and rutting arenas.

Red deer are creatures of mature woodland, open farmland and open hills (such as the Highlands of Scotland). While they habitually feed in favoured areas, red deer tend to approach their feeding grounds through many different

SIZE
Male (stag) larger than female (hind)
Weight: 120–170kg (exceptionally large stags up to 500kg)
Length to rump: 1.8–2m
Height at shoulder: 95cm–1.3m

Front foot often over-stepped with rear print

Long, large and with rounded ends to toes

On hard ground, very little gap between the toes

routes and do not necessarily create well-worn paths in any but the most regularly visited sites, such as artificial feeding stations or salt licks. Exceptions to this occur where red deer are offered supplementary feeding and so come and go from a single feeding site time and again, creating worn paths. The size and form of their footprints in any bare soil on these paths should establish their owner's identity.

In the build up to and during the rut and, less frequently, at other times of year, red deer take to wallows. These are areas of wet, marshy ground with soft mud or peat. The deer – more often stags than hinds, though both sexes wallow from time to time – scrape away at a shallow depression or puddle until there is bare earth and water mixed. They then lie and roll in the depression until they are partly or entirely covered in the wet mud or peat.

When wallows are used in the rutting season the stags often urinate in them, and the musky pungent scent is easy for the human nose to detect. Several different stags and occasionally hinds will use the same wallow. The muddy depressions are often characterised by deep scratches made by the animals' cloven hooves scraping the banks, as well as marks made by the stags' antlers as they roll and twist in the mud.

The males (and some females) of most deer species go through the process of growing and casting antlers each year. Old antlers fall off and new ones grow, covered by a furry skin known as velvet. Once the antlers reach full size, the skin dies off and is scraped clean on branches and other vegetation. This process ensures that even if an antler breaks during a fight, deer have a full set of antlers the following year.

Fraying stocks are created when the stags rid their antlers of velvet in the early autumn, usually by rubbing them against the tangled low branches of trees like sallow or on the fallen branches of more substantial trees such as oak or ash. Within a short time, the bark from these branches is stripped back, leaving them tattered and naked. Even when their antlers are clean of velvet, stags still thrash at branches, bracken, rushes

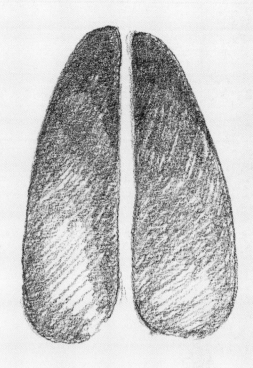

Front right print of adult stag (actual size)

and tall grass. This often results in areas of vegetation being beaten down and torn from its roots – and the stag sporting a rather fetching headdress of tangled vegetation for a while! Thrashing is often accompanied by urinating, and so the musky scent of a stag in rut can be detected close to the thrashed area.

Red deer rut on traditional patches of ground known as stands. These are unlike those used by some other species of deer, however, as they are loosely held patches – frequently places to which the hinds are attracted to feed on nutritious grass or other foodstuffs. Each stag patrols and defends an area that may cover several hundred square metres, and the boundaries to such a stand are often quite variable. Stags are very vociferous during the rut and regularly roar from the middle and the edges of their chosen ground. See page 87 for more on red deer vocalisations.

FAECES *Droppings or fewmets*

The roughly cylindrical, bean-shaped droppings measure 2–2.5cm long and 13–18cm thick. The colour is blackish to dark brown or dark olive green (depending on the diet of the deer). Like other deer droppings, these often have a small nipple at one end and a shallow depression on the other. This is especially true of droppings produced during the winter months, when the diet mostly consists of dry grasses. During the summer months, the change to wetter food produces clumps of droppings that may stick together. All deer droppings are covered in a thin, shiny mucus when very fresh but this dries quickly – the exact time this takes depends on the weather and temperature on the day.

FOOD REMAINS

This species feeds predominantly on grasses and the leaves of low-hanging tree branches and wildflowers. They graze and browse widely and, apart from tree damage, there are rarely any clear feeding signs that can be attributed specifically to them.

HAIR

Red deer hair is long, thick and quite coarse, being roughly ovoid in cross section. It varies in colour depending on the

Red deer droppings vary according to the amount of moisture in the diet. Dry fewmets are large and bean shaped, with a nipple at one end and a dimple at the other [TOP]. Wetter droppings form clusters, often compressed into small mounds [ABOVE].

Red deer are armed with an acute battery of senses and they are able to hear, smell and spot a human at significant distances.

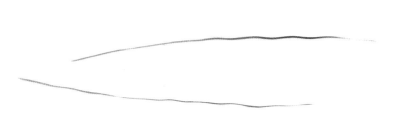

Red deer hair is long and thick. The base is a pale grey-brown, becoming a darker russet colour towards the tip. Most hairs end in a darker point. Each hair is gently corrugated along its length and is ovoid in cross section.

time of year. Body hairs are pale grey at the base, becoming increasingly reddish brown towards the tip in summer. In winter, the tip is grey-brown.

During spring (April/May) red deer moult their winter coat and leave large clumps of hair where they have been resting or grooming. The hair is a favourite material of jackdaws for lining their nest cups and the birds may collect it directly from a resting or grazing deer.

HOW TO WATCH

Many royal and other parks in the UK keep herds of red deer as an ornamental and land management addition to the estate. Richmond Park in London famously has a large red deer herd which is easily observed, since the animals are so used to the presence of benign humans.

Wild deer populations are generally much more nervous due to their negative encounters with humans. Just how nervous a deer population is depends on the animals' experiences of encountering our species.

When watching a nervous population, wind direction, sound and human form must all be taken into consideration. Use existing features such as trees, rocks and folds in the land to camouflage your outline.

A field hide (page 24) may be useful in places the deer visits regularly – for example, at a wallow or rutting stand. During periods outside the rut, adult male and female deer live apart, forming bachelor herds and hind and calf herds. The fidelity shown by individual stags to one another during these periods is remarkably consistent; the same individuals spend the best part of the year together, year after year, despite the fact that they become arch enemies during the months of the rut. Females too, tend to hang out together in known groups, though these allegiances are not as well defined as those of the stags.

RED DEER'S YEAR

Antlers growing in velvet: March–late August (earlier for mature stags)

Hard antlers: late August–March

Antlers cast: March–May (older stags cast first)

Breeding/rut: September/October

Gestation: 233–236 days

Young: usually 1 calf born May/June; rarely twins

[OPPOSITE] A stag finds his voice during the annual rut, roaring repeatedly to assert his prowess and draw hinds to his rutting stand.

RED DEER SENSES

Sound
10

Sight
9

Smell
10

Red deer stags are easy to pinpoint during the rut due to their loud roars. If you have identified an active stand, move into your watching position at or just before first light and be patient. Even if the stag moves off as you arrive, he, or another deer, is likely to return once it feels the coast is clear.

Stags respond to the mimicry of another roaring stag or to the sound of clashing antlers, which may signify a fight close to their stand. The volume and depth of a red deer stag roar is such that it is difficult to replicate accurately other than by the most sonorous and bass of male voices. It helps to use a short length of plastic pipe, about 5cm in diameter, to roar down to add to the resonance. Hinds and calves may be watched throughout the summer months on their feeding grounds, and calves form crèches with several youngsters running and playing together, most often on a clear evening.

ROE DEER *Capreolus capreolus*

SIGN
FOOTPRINTS
The size of roe deer tracks distinguishes them those of most other deer species – smaller than red, fallow and sika; larger than muntjac and Chinese water deer. Their fine form and teardrop shape, with sharply pointed toe tips, separate them from those of sheep and goats, which have a more plump-looking toe, with a less pointed tip. On hard ground the toes are kept close together; on soft they are splayed with the tips spread wide. In the latter condition, the dewclaw of the forefoot may also leave a mark. On very hard ground, only the toe tips show, looking like two narrow 'V's side by side.

OTHER SIGN
Key roe deer sign, besides their footprints, are paths, scrapes, lies, fraying stocks and rutting rings.

Roe paths are often made by the repeated traffic of several individuals, using the same track through a woodland or hedgerow, on their way to and from favoured feeding or resting points. A diagnostic feature of a roe path is their footprints in softer ground, but where the deer move

SIZE
Male (buck) larger than female (doe)
Weight: 15–35kg
Length to rump: 95cm–1.35m
Height at shoulder: 65–75cm

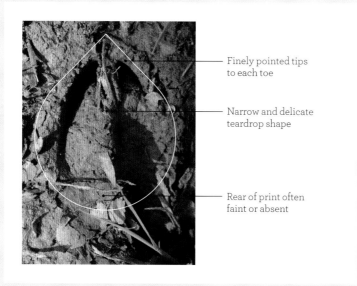

Finely pointed tips to each toe

Narrow and delicate teardrop shape

Rear of print often faint or absent

Front left print (actual size)

In winter, roe often feed and rest together in mature buck and doe pairs. Larger groups usually include the young from the previous summer.

In wet soil the toes are splayed to spread the deer's weight load.

through thick cover, the height of the 'tunnel' also indicates that it is used by roe, where it is consistently higher than 50cm but lower than a metre or so (see Muntjac page 110).

Roe scrapes are made almost exclusively by bucks, and are frequently found at the base of fraying stocks. These scrapes occur where the buck scratches repeatedly at the ground, often clearing it of all leaves and twigs, and leaving characteristic double score lines made by the toes of the cloven hoof. These scrapes may bear the scent of the buck (which has scent glands between its toes), but this is not discernible to the human nose.

Fraying stocks are made by bucks when they are cleaning their antlers of velvet and while scent marking around their territory. They choose young trees with vertical or near vertical trunks; anything from 1cm up to 5 or 6cm in diameter (with a distinct preference for trees about 2cm in diameter). The bucks rub their antlers, and the skin on their head between their antlers, up and down these stocks repeatedly, stripping the tree of its bark on one side, and sometimes around its entire circumference killing the tree above this point.

The lowest point of such fraying is usually about 30cm from the ground; the highest point is rarely higher than a metre. Fraying stocks are used most vigorously from March through to August.

Roe often choose to rest in the same patch of woodland or field edge, but are not faithful to a specific site. A 'lie' may be made afresh each day, and can be identified by an area of flattened vegetation (such as grass and bluebells) and often a small patch of ground that has been scraped bare. Droppings may be found very close to, or on the edge of a lie.

When roe deer rut, the buck closely follows the doe, and the pair may trot in a tight circle or figure of eight. This is how 'roe rings' are created, since the wear on the ground from the hooves of the deer flattens vegetation and may wear a clear path. In woodland settings, these roe rings may be worn around a bush or patch of trees but they also occur in open fields. They are usually no more than about 4–5 metres in diameter.

Patches of ground scraped clear of vegetation with the surrounding foliage flattened are typical of lies made by adult roe. Bucks tend to clear the vegetation by scraping with their forefeet more vigorously than does.

FAECES *Droppings or fewmets*
Most deer droppings have a roughly similar form, and their size and location give the best indication of species. Roe droppings are about 1cm long, 0.5cm across and bean shaped. One end bears a distinctive nipple, the other a shallow depression. As the droppings are formed in the rectum, they line up and fit together – nipple into depression until they are passed and fall singly to the floor. Depending on the deer's diet, they may sometimes clump together and form a more coherent mass, but on close inspection the size and form of each dropping is usually apparent.

FOOD REMAINS
Roe are browsing deer and they nibble from a wide variety of vegetation. In open fields they often target the heads of dandelion, clover and other flowers. A very careful, close inspection of flower stems that have had their heads removed suggests roe feeding behaviour. The same applies to garden flowers, particularly roses, much to the chagrin of some gardeners! On woodland edge roe favour the leaves of bramble and other low shrubs, but it is extremely difficult to attribute browsing of this nature to roe in particular,

Roe deer droppings [ABOVE LEFT] are narrow and bean shaped, with a point at one end and a dimple at the other. Compare them with sheep droppings [ABOVE RIGHT] which are a similar size but more rounded and usually form large clusters.

since other deer will do the same. Roe also nibble the tops from young trees from time to time – a cause of conflict with the forestry industry.

HAIR

Roe hair is distinctive and may be found in clumps during the late spring when the deer are moulting into their summer coat, or snagged on barbed wire fences in places where the deer jump, or duck under the wire. Hair colour varies according to the season – grey brown in winter, russet in summer and which part of the body it is from. The coat is longer in winter and more likely to be found during the spring moult and snagged on fences. A close inspection of the hair reveals a corrugated form and coarse base with a finer tip that tends to be paler than the rest of the hair.

HOME

The only 'home' as such of this, or any other British deer species, is their lie, described on page 90.

Roe frequently lose hair as they jump over or push through barbed wire fences. Hair colour depends on which part of the animal it has been plucked from, and the time of year.

[RIGHT] Back hair from a winter buck. Each hair is corrugated to a greater or lesser extent and varies from light to dark along its length. The summer coat contains more red pigment.

HOW TO WATCH

Roe, like most deer species in the UK, are hunted by humans and are generally very nervous of any sign that people are nearby.

The tradition in shooting circles of using a high seat to target deer exploits the fact that most deer rarely look much above the horizon for danger and so are less likely to spot trouble in the trees (or their man-made equivalent).

Roe deer are creatures of habit when undisturbed, and a careful reading and understanding of their sign will help establish the best places to watch for them. Certain fields, rich in flowers, attract roe in the early morning and late evening to feed. Staking out one of these field borders, using a hide or making a field hide (page 24), is a good method for close views. Remember that these animals have an incredibly acute sense of smell, so wind direction is of critical importance in all observation approaches.

While it is possible to 'stalk' deer, their acute hearing makes it almost impossible to get very close without them hearing your footfall on a twig or leaf. Fine if you only want to get to within 50 metres or so, but useless for close prolonged observation of behaviour. Staking out with a hide of sorts also works well along well-used deer tracks or paths in woodland, as well as overlooking fraying stocks. Ensure that your hide outline is camouflaged by an existing natural feature, such as a bush or hedgerow, or even man-made features that the deer are used to, such as stacks of hay bales.

In the summer months, the does give birth, often to twins. For the first few weeks of life, these young (known as kids or fawns in roe deer) are left alone in long grass or other thick cover for hours on end. If the doe feels the coast is clear, she returns to her young to suckle them in the early morning and late evening. If you suspect that there are young in a field, leave them well alone, and, mindful of the wind direction, stake out the scene using the methods described above. Few sights are more lovely than roe kids charging to and fro around the meadow's edge like little delicate lambs.

If a roe gets very close to your hiding place it may stop and stare directly at you for a short while, then go back to browsing. Do not be fooled – remain completely motionless even when the deer goes back to feeding. There is a very

ROE DEER'S YEAR

Antlers growing in velvet: October–March

Hard antlers: late March–October (mature bucks may cast antlers earlier)

Antlers cast: October/November (older bucks cast first)

Breeding/rut: July/August

Gestation: 196 days – implantation is delayed for 4 months; full gestation occurs from late December/early January onwards

Young: kids born in May/June; usually twins

ROE DEER SENSES

Sound	Sight	Smell
10	9	10

Roe deer gender can be established with a view of their rump patch. On a doe [ABOVE], this is like an upside-down heart, with a tuft of hair (not a tail) running from the centre. The buck (page 88) has a kidney-shaped rump and no anal tuft.

strong chance the same animal will suddenly lift its head to stare straight at you once again, trying to catch you off guard and establish your identity. After a couple of these 'false relaxes', the deer will either move gently away or else settle, confident that you are not a threat.

In common with many nervous wild animals, roe may watch you passing by from the security of a woodland edge at fairly close proximity, as long as they do not feel they have been spotted. If you spot a deer under these circumstances deploy the 'disinterested' observation technique (page 17).

Roe deer are surprisingly vocal, but many of the sounds they make are very low volume or of a frequency that makes them hard for the human ear to perceive.

In stalking circles, squeaking up a roe buck is a tried and tested method during the rut to bring male (and female) deer running in the direction of the person making the sound, and whistles and hand-held squeakers are commercially available for this purpose. For observation (as opposed to stalking), this technique has limited value, however, since once the deer has come close enough to discover that there is no other deer in the area, but instead a human, views are usually brief (albeit close) and end with the deer running off in the opposite direction in fear. Even if the 'caller' is well hidden and the approaching

deer remains ignorant of a human presence, views tend to be of an animal searching for the source of the sound and rarely mature into more natural behaviour.

The sound produced by the whistle is a high-pitched squeak, and this is emitted by the user in relatively short duration 'peeps', one or two in fairly rapid succession, with fairly long gaps between each sequence. Having watched roe rutting many times, I have doubts as to whether this sound is produced by a doe to attract a buck, as is often cited in stalking literature. Instead the sound may come from her distressed kids which, for the first time in their lives, find their mother otherwise occupied by the attentions of an attendant buck and so call for her attention. I have certainly had rapid and marked responses from roe bucks and does when I have imitated this 'kid call'. Based solely on my observations (as opposed to existing literature), I assume that bucks recognise the call of the kids as a sign that a doe is being pursued by another buck and so come running to investigate.
I have never watched a doe walking alone and making this call.

At very close proximity, a buck following the scent of a doe in the rut can be heard to gently grunt or rasp, but I have never found mimicry of this sound to be an asset in observation.

At all times of year, roe produce an explosive bark if they are alarmed. This deep, chesty sound is uttered several times in a row and often as the animal stotts away in the opposite direction. Rather than confirming that the deer has spotted you, this sound suggests it has become nervous but is uncertain of where or what the danger may be. It could be that it has caught a whiff of your scent or that it has heard a twig break beneath your foot, but it has not established that you are a real threat. If you hear this barking, remain still and quiet and wait for it to subside before continuing your observations.

A very similar call is produced by both bucks and does as some form of communication call. To the untrained ear, it really does sound very like an alarm bark, but it lacks the explosive urgency of the latter, and may continue with several phrases longer than when alarmed.

Buck especially produce this call leading up to and around the rut and, with practice, mimicking the bark can pique the interest of a territorial male. I produce it by inhaling sharply across my vocal cords, keeping my jaw slightly open and forming an 'O' with my lips. Roe buck and doe have come towards my hiding place when they have heard my attempt at their language, although at times, they have ignored me completely. I remain uncertain as to the significance of the calls as far as roe social life is concerned.

A young roe doe. This species is equipped with sharp senses and will take flight at the first hint of danger.

FALLOW DEER *Dama dama*

SIGN
FOOTPRINTS
The hoof prints of most deer species are more or less similar and fallow are no exception. They are distinguished from other British species by size (between adult roe and red deer) and by a slightly heavier-looking heel. Their 'toes' are a little less pointed than the similarly sized sika. Prints on hard ground will reveal the toes close together; those on soft ground will often have splayed toes and may, if the deer slips, also show marks of the dewclaw.

OTHER SIGN
Key fallow deer sign, besides their footprints, are paths, scrapes, lies, fraying stocks and rutting stands.

In common with roe and sika deer, fallow use favoured paths through woodland and when entering open country to feed. Their footprints and droppings on the bare earth of these paths positively identifies their presence.

As they approach breeding condition and throughout the rut, fallow bucks create areas scraped clear of leaves and other vegetation, using their forefeet. These are often made

SIZE
Male (buck) larger than female (doe)
Weight: 60–100kg
Length to rump: 1.4–1.6m
Height at shoulder: 85–95cm

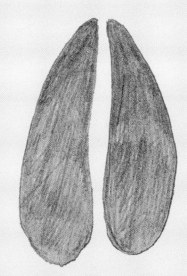

Front left print (actual size)

[OPPOSITE] A mature fallow buck in full breeding condition. Note the extended Adam's apple, powerfully muscled neck and narrow waist. Compare him with the summer buck on page 101.

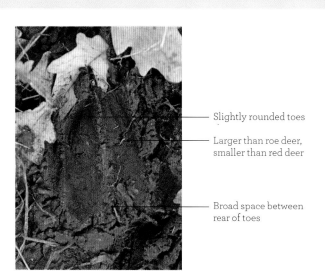

Slightly rounded toes

Larger than roe deer, smaller than red deer

Broad space between rear of toes

just before the buck lies down in the middle of the bare patch, or more rarely, while they are fraying a branch or tree trunk. These scrapes lack the triangular form created by roe deer and tend to be more oval in shape. While the bucks frequently urinate on the bare earth before they lie down, fallow rutting scent is less powerful and rather sweeter to the nose than red deer scent.

As the bucks' antlers harden off in the late summer, so the velvet skin dies and is frayed off by rubbing up against anything from low branches to fence posts and tree trunks. Little shreds of the skin may be found hanging in low branches or on the ground beneath a tree trunk where the deer has repeatedly scraped up against it.

In the rut, the bucks find their voice and begin to emit loud barks or grunts (which I think sound more like someone producing a very loud belch than a bark). They make about one per second, in bursts of one to four or five in a row. If a buck has spotted a group of does or they are moving through his rutting stand, he will get particularly noisy, with barely any gap between bursts of grunts. This makes it very easy to establish if a rutting buck is in a territory. Even without this audible aid, rutting bucks leave lots of evidence of their activity.

[ABOVE LEFT] Fallen branches or low shrubs are used for fraying – scraping the antlers against the surface. This starts as the bucks lose the velvet from their antlers in late summer and continues up to and throughout the rut. Favoured branches are scraped clean of bark and may take on a polished appearance.

[ABOVE RIGHT] Scrapes on the ground made by bucks are rounded and likely to bear footprints and hair [SEE INSERT].

A stand is a patch of ground that is often, but not always, in woodland and to which a buck may return year after year to attract females with a view to mating. Some of the most successful bucks choose stands in areas that also have good forage for the does, such as acorns or other mast (fruit of forest trees). Bucks rarely eat at the height of the rut. Around the edges of the stand, the buck frequently thrashes vegetation and scrapes the ground (page 98) and these signs of wear are clues that there has been recent activity. Unlike red and sika deer, fallow do not create wallows.

In places where the population is dense, bucks may form something more akin to a lek (as do birds such as black grouse and ruff) than a discrete rutting stand. Several bucks will grunt and strut in very close proximity to each other in open country, all vying for the attention of the does. This happens in some English parks (such as Petworth Park in West Sussex) and in parts of the fallow's original range in the eastern Mediterranean and southern Europe. Large areas of trampled ground can be seen at these lekking sites.

Where fallow rest, they may compress vegetation like bracken into a neat couch that takes on the shape of their body. Only the presence of droppings, hair or footprints will confirm the identity of the creature that made the bed with certainty, however.

FAECES *Droppings or fewmets*
Fallow deer droppings are intermediate in size between those of roe and red deer, measuring 10–15mm long by 8–11mm wide. They share similar characteristics – bean shaped, often with a nipple one end and a depression at the other – but are frequently coarser looking than the shiny black droppings of a roe deer, with visible vegetation in the mix.

FOOD REMAINS
In common with other deer species, fallow browse, forage and graze, depending on the seasonal availability of food. They may have an impact on forestry and agricultural crops if they feed on these in large numbers.

Use the usual clues of footprints, hair and so on to establish which species has caused any deer feeding sign.

Fallow droppings are larger than those of the roe, smaller than red, and usually more rounded and coarser than either. Typically, each has a dimple in one end and a nipple on the other.

Fallow are particularly partial to fallen mast, including sweet and horse chestnuts. They will pick these up in their mouths, complete with spiny outer casing, crack into the nut within using their molars and allow the husk to fall to the floor. The discarded husks litter the ground beneath the tree and may be wet with saliva if fresh. Some bucks learn to use their antlers to access food they might not otherwise be able to reach, such as low-hanging apples. They rear up on their hind legs and knock the fruit down with the tips of their antlers. Such feeding creates a litter of leaves and broken twigs beneath the tree, together with fragments of chewed apples that have fallen from the mouths of the bucks.

HAIR

Fallow deer come in several different colour morphs which they maintain throughout their lives. These are broadly separated into four distinct types known as common, menil, black and white. Add to this the darker winter coat of the common morph and you have a bewildering range of hair colour! Fallow deer hair lacks the corrugations of roe deer hair and is less coarse than red deer hair. Oval in cross section, it tends to be found in clumps during the spring moult where deer have been resting or grooming, or where it has snagged on or close to wire fences. Like red deer hair, it is a common component in the lining of birds' nests.

HOW TO WATCH

Fallow deer herds are commonly managed in large parks and estates as semi-wild stock which are enjoyed for ornamental purposes and culled annually for their meat. These animals are often very familiar with humans and, though they are shot at from time to time, the vast majority of their encounters with people are benign. As a result they can be remarkably approachable. Elsewhere, truly 'wild' fallow tend to prefer mature woodland with access to open

Fallow hair colour can be extremely variable and is coarser than roe deer hair, finer than red deer. This example from the back of a buck in winter reveals the pale base, darker reddish-brown mid section, broad pale sub-terminal band and dark tip. Most clumps contain some whiter hairs.

FALLOW DEER'S YEAR

Antlers growing in velvet: May–August

Hard antlers: mid August–April

Antlers cast: late March–early May (older bucks cast first)

Breeding/rut: September–November (peak around 21 October)

Gestation: 229 days

Young: usually a single fawn born in June

Bucks form bachelor herds in summer. They fatten up on rich grazing and browse, while their antlers grow beneath the protective layer of velvet skin. Come the rut, these bucks will become arch rivals.

fields for nocturnal grazing. These populations are often much more nervous of humans than their parkland cousins.

Bucks remain in bachelor herds throughout the spring and summer, and the does and fawns generally don't mix with mature males at these times. During the approach to the rut, a buck goes through an astonishing series of physical changes – his neck thickens, his waistline shrinks and his antlers harden off and lose the velvet skin that has nourished them throughout their annual growth period.

Watching wild fallow rutting is a truly thrilling experience; the sound and sight of bucks vying for the attention of the does, sometimes locking antlers in combat for those rights, is high-octane natural theatre. Since the bucks generally keep to well-established rutting stands, the best method for close observation is to build a field hide (page 24). Build your hide on the margins of a known

FALLOW DEER SENSES

Sound	Sight	Smell
10	9	10

rutting stand (not smack bang in the middle of it) a day or two before your planned day of observation, then return and settle into it before first light. You may disturb a deer or two as you arrive, but if you have paid attention to all the other observation rules, such as wind direction, camouflage and movement, you should be in for a treat.

In places where wild fallow are artificially fed on a regular basis you can get great views of herds that have become accustomed to a set pattern of human behaviour. Remember though that these are still wild deer, and anything out of the ordinary is likely to spook them. It is uncanny how habituated herds will accept children screaming and crowds of folk watching them from a viewing platform, but just one human walking in an unexpected place can send the whole mob running!

Rutting fallow bucks respond to mimicry of grunts and the sound of antlers clashing, but I have found neither method of much aid to prolonged observation of the animals' natural behaviour.

[OPPOSITE TOP] During the rut, bucks attract does to their stand, grunting, strutting and posturing to gain their favour.

[OPPOSITE BELOW] Bucks fight furiously to defend prime rutting stands. Battles involve the combatants locking antlers and using their speed, agility, strength and weight to try to exhaust and wrong-foot their opponent.

[RIGHT] Rutting mature bucks grunt, making a sound like a loud belch, and pace around their rutting stand. Does may be attracted to the fittest males.

SIKA DEER *Cervus nippon*

SIGN

FOOTPRINTS

Sika slots are very similar to those of fallow deer (page 96) in both form and size. They appear a little more pointed than a fallow's and in many individuals, marginally narrower.

OTHER SIGN

Sika are native to Japan and southeast China (including Taiwan). They were first introduced to Ireland in 1860, and thereafter to many other parts of the British Isles. Subsequent escapes and intentional releases have led to a fully naturalised population. The behaviour of British sika is influenced by the habitat in which they live. They are essentially woodland deer, but will adapt to more open habitats.

Key sign, besides their footprints, are wallows, scrapes, lies and fraying stocks.

Where sika are common, trails to and from their favoured feeding grounds can become pronounced, particularly where they cross a field border or ditch. These look very like the

SIZE
Male (stag) larger than
female (hind)
Weight: 32–63kg
Length to rump: 1.38–1.8m
Height at shoulder: 50cm–1.2m

Narrower, more pointed toes than fallow deer

Smaller than red deer

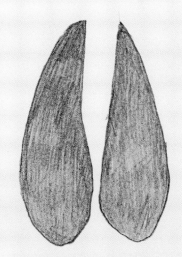

Stag front left print (actual size)

[OPPOSITE] A sika hind in autumn/ winter coat. In summer, both male and female are reddish with white spots.

[OPPOSITE TOP RIGHT] In common with many deer species, a sika stag creates some of the most distinctive sign in the build-up to and during the autumn rut.

[OPPOSITE TOP LEFT] Wallows are scraped in wet soil, often in woodland. Stags urinate in the wallow and roll in the muddy, scented mixture.

[OPPOSITE CENTRE LEFT] Stags fray areas of vegetation like this bracken, and scrape the ground bare with their forefeet.

[OPPOSITE BOTTOM LEFT] Fallen trees and large branches are used as fraying stocks.

[OPPOSITE BOTTOM RIGHT] A close look reveals deep gouges made by the tines on a stag's antlers as they scrape against the wood.

Droppings are similar in size and form to those of a fallow deer, but each pellet is more rounded.

trails created by fallow deer and even the presence of footprints and droppings may require visual confirmation of the creature that made them before you can be confident that sika were involved.

Unlike fallow, sika stags regularly wallow in the prelude to and during the rut, and may also create wet, muddy scrapes at other times of year. I have found active sika wallows in late summer. They look very like red deer wallows (page 83) though are often a little smaller, reflecting the size of the animal that made them. The scent left in and around the wallow is less heady and of a sweeter musk than that of red deer (though to identify the difference the observer does, of course, need to know what a red deer wallow smells like for comparison!).

For details of thrashing and fraying behaviour, and the ensuing damage to vegetation, see Red deer (page 83). The sign left by the two species is almost impossible to tell apart, though tracks in wet ground surrounding the activity should act as a guide.

Sika rutting behaviour is similar to that of red deer, though the stags are often more dynamic in their movement around traditional rutting areas. Stands may occur within woodland, on woodland edge or open fields, and the borders of a stag's claimed rutting stand usually include some natural or man-made feature such as a fence line, hedge or ditch. These borders may see a lot of traffic during the rut, as stags patrol up and down, frequently walking in parallel on either side of a physical or imaginary border and leaving paths of worn vegetation or bare ground heavily pitted with their slots.

FAECES *Droppings or fewmets*
Sika deer droppings are intermediate in size between roe and red deer but are virtually indistinguishable from fallow deer droppings in the field. Like fallow droppings, they measure about 10–15mm long by 8–11mm wide but are slightly more rounded. They share similar characteristics, being bean shaped, often with a nipple at one end and a depression at the other. They are frequently coarser looking than the smaller, shiny black droppings of a roe deer, with visible vegetation in the mix.

FOOD REMAINS

Sika leave little or no species-specific sign that they have been feeding. Much of the evidence looks very like that left by fallow (page 99) or red deer (page 85).

HAIR

Like many deer, this species undergoes a dramatic change in pelage from summer to autumn/winter. During the warmer months and longer days, sika have a patterning which resembles the common-phase fallow summer coat, though the base colour is more a dark reddish-brown with white spots instead of the yellow-brown of the fallow. In autumn and winter sika develop a darker, plain coat of dark grey-brown. This can appear almost black in the stags, especially after wallowing. Accordingly, sika hair is very variable.

HOW TO WATCH

Observation techniques vary according to habitat and time of year. I have spent a great deal of time watching and filming sika in forest habitats and have used the sit-and-wait method from a field hide (page 24) and more active approaches both on foot and using a vehicle as a hide on forest rides. In more open habitats, such as pasture fields and heaths, field hides or very careful mobile camouflage are successful. At all times wind direction and sound must be considered, especially in areas where sika are regularly shot at (which is almost everywhere they occur). Like other deer species, sika tend to be crepuscular or nocturnal, so observations before first light and approaching dusk are likely to be most successful.

Identifying a good position for a field hide depends on the habitat and behaviour of the deer you are hoping to watch. During the rut, stags draw attention to themselves with some of the most varied and striking vocalisations of any deer species, making sounds ranging from piercing whistles to groans that sound like a person suffering torture. These can help you choose an appropriate location to set up a hide. Three major calls predominate during the rut: the tri-whistle, the whistle-groan and chuckling.

[TOP] Hair varies in colour depending on the time of year and the part of the body it has come from. This back hair from an autumnal animal is pale grey at the base and reddish-brown along much of its length, with a darker tip. It has less obvious corrugations than roe, fallow or red deer hair.

[ABOVE] Hair is often snagged on barbed wire fences where deer move in and out of favoured feeding sites. Paths at these sites become well worn.

SIKA DEER'S YEAR

Antlers growing in velvet: April–August

Hard antlers: mid-August–March

Antlers cast: late March/April (older bucks cast first)

Breeding/rut: September–November

Gestation: 217 days

Young: usually 1 calf, born early May/late June

SIKA DEER SENSES

Sound
10

Sight
9

Smell
10

Sika are forest deer, though in the UK many graze in open fields, especially at dusk, dawn and through the night. In areas where they are undisturbed they can be very confiding.

The tri-whistle, as the name suggests, consists of three piercing whistles, each of which rises and falls with barely a second between one and the next and is generally uttered by a stag on the move through his home patch. Rarely, if ever, does this call lead you to a male deer that has already secured a harem.

The contrary is true of the whistle groan – a long, drawn-out call that starts with a piercingly high whistle and ends with a human-like groan. This is usually uttered by a stag that has secured a stand and harem and is reinforcing his claims.

The chuckle, which again bears uncanny resemblance to a demonic human voice, is made when one stag chases another and is a good indicator of antagonistic behaviour. Hinds with calves make low-intensity reedy calls and are particularly vociferous when being harried by a stag. These sounds carry through forest and over fields and if heard, wind direction and cover should be carefully considered before making any move towards them.

MUNTJAC *Muntiacus reevesi*

SIGN

FOOTPRINTS

The small size (about 3cm or less in length) of this typical cloven hoof print sets it apart from all but the young of other deer and possibly Chinese water deer. Toes are asymmetric, with one longer than the other.

OTHER SIGN

Muntjac keep a low profile and may live in large gardens without being seen. They browse on herbage and have a fondness for the leaves and flowers of ornamental roses. Where they are undisturbed muntjac use habitual paths from resting sites to feeding areas. These runs form tunnels through dense vegetation and are about 40cm high and rounded in appearance.

Muntjac are very vocal – their other name is the barking deer. They bark repeatedly if alarmed, when a doe is contacting her young or especially during the protracted breeding season, which runs throughout the year but may peak from late summer to late spring. Barks are dog-like, but repeated at intervals of about two seconds and may go on for many minutes. Does squeak when being pursued by a buck, and fawns produce very high-pitched squeaks when calling their mother.

SIZE
Male (buck) slightly larger than female (doe)
Weight: 15kg
Length to rump: 50cm
Height at shoulder: 50cm

Buck front right print (actual size)

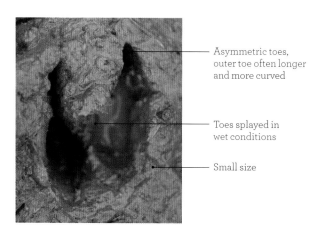

Asymmetric toes, outer toe often longer and more curved

Toes splayed in wet conditions

Small size

Droppings are smaller than those of rabbits, bean shaped and glossy black.

MUNTJAC SENSES

Sound	Sight	Smell
10	9	8

MUNTJAC'S YEAR

Muntjacs are a non-native tropical species and lack the strict seasonality of native deer. They are unique among UK deer in being able to breed throughout the year.

FAECES *Droppings or fewmets*

Droppings are about 1cm long. Each dropping usually has a slight dimple at one end and a point at the other, but at certain times of year, and depending on diet, they may be rounded at both ends or clumped. When eating a wet diet, muntjac produce clumps of droppings

HAIR

Most of the body hair is a rich russet red, with little or no corrugation. It is coarser than fox hair.

HOW TO WATCH

The methods used to observe roe deer broadly apply to this species. Mimicry of barking can successfully draw both buck and doe close to the observer, and mimicry of fawn squeaks may also draw both sexes close by.

[ABOVE TOP LEFT] A day couch made by a resting muntjac.

[ABOVE BOTTOM LEFT] Runs and grass tunnels are made by passing muntjac. These are 40–50cm high.

[ABOVE RIGHT] Muntjac bucks are stocky and hunch-backed. The tiny antlers are set on long pedicles.

[LEFT] Muntjac hair is fine, soft and lacks corrugation. Main body hairs have a pale grey base, blending towards dark brown near the end. There is a sub-terminal pale reddish band before the dark tip.

CHINESE WATER DEER *Hydropotes inermis*

This is the only deer species found in the UK in which the bucks do not have antlers. They do, however, have pronounced tusks which protrude as fangs (see opposite).

SIGN
FOOTPRINTS
The hind foot of this deer is adapted for moving through damp, marshy ground, with long relatively narrow toes, each of which bears a slight kink. When well splayed, these leave a distinctive slot. The forefoot is 3–4cm wide, 4–5cm long and similar to that of a muntjac, often with asymmetric toes. Hind footprints often overstep fore footprints. Among deer species in the UK, only the muntjac leaves a marginally smaller print.

OTHER SIGN
Chinese water deer feed largely on grasses, sedges and herbaceous plants and they leave nibbled stems. It is virtually impossible to determine which deer species has grazed on them. Well-worn runs to and from favoured

SIZE
Male (buck) very slightly larger than female (doe)
Weight: 11–18kg
Length to rump: 75cm–1m
Height at shoulder: 45–55cm

Rear left print (actual size)

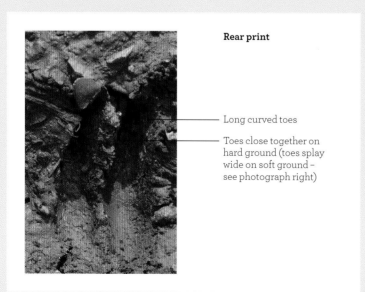

Rear print

Long curved toes

Toes close together on hard ground (toes splay wide on soft ground – see photograph right)

The long toes of the rear foot have been partly obscured by the front footprint.

Droppings are produced in clusters which may or may not fall apart into pellets, depending on the moisture level. Look for dimples in the sides of the pellets.

feeding areas may pass through fence and hedge lines and here, especially during the spring moult, hair may be found. This is long, very pale from the root along the majority of the hair shaft, terminating in a yellowish-brown tip. There is a darker band close to the end of each hair.

FAECES *Droppings or fewmets*
Like many deer droppings, these are bean shaped, with a distinct nipple at one end and a dimple on the other. They are about 1cm long. If clumps become separated the droppings often bear dimples on the sides – these are formed when the droppings are compressed together as they are excreted. Droppings may be found in litters of single pellets or clumped, depending on the moisture level in the diet.

WATER DEER SENSES

Sound	Sight	Smell
10	**9**	**10**

HOW TO WATCH

This is a solitary species, and the bucks are fiercely territorial for the most part.

In their restricted range in the UK, they are relatively easy to watch, becoming more active at dusk and dawn, though potentially feeding at any time of day or night. See roe deer (page 92) for observation techniques.

CHINESE WATER DEER'S YEAR
These bucks do not have antlers
Mating/rut: November/December
Gestation: 180–210 days
Young: up to 5 (usually 2 or 3) fawns born in May/June

[OPPOSITE] Mature does do not have the extended tusks of the bucks. Furry ears and face, button eyes and nose give them a 'teddy bear' look.

[RIGHT] Hair is thick, heavily corrugated and long. Most body hair is pale grey at the base and stem, turning dark brown near the tip. There is a pale yellow-tan sub-terminal band before the small dark tip.

WILD BOAR *Sus scrofa*

SIGN

FOOTPRINTS

The boar's broad, heavy, cloven-hoofed track is usually accompanied by dewclaw imprints (deer rarely leave these). In wild boar, dewclaw prints sit wider than the hoof print, giving the entire spoor a trapezoid outline. If deer do leave dewclaw marks, they sit behind the main hoof, creating a more rectangular outline.

The size of the boar's track is very variable, depending on the gender and age of the animal; adult males leave the largest track, while piglets make delicate little prints which may not have dewclaw marks. An average adult print measures about 7cm long.

FAECES *Droppings*

Boar droppings vary a great deal depending on diet and are indistinguishable from those of domestic swine that have been feeding on the same materials. When the boar has been feeding on wet vegetation, droppings may be very loose, almost like those of a bovid. More commonly, they are a tight cluster of roughly spherical

SIZE
Male (boar) much larger than female (sow)
Weight: 80–175kg
Length to rump: 90cm–1.8m
Tail length: 15–40cm
Height at shoulder: 55cm–1.1m

Front foot of adult male

Large, broad, heavy cloven hoof

Dewclaws usually leave a mark

Droppings are very variable in consistency, depending on the boar's diet. Wetter dung forms clumped clusters [ABOVE]. Drier dung, which is more typical, forms dark flattened pellets of varying size and shape [TOP].

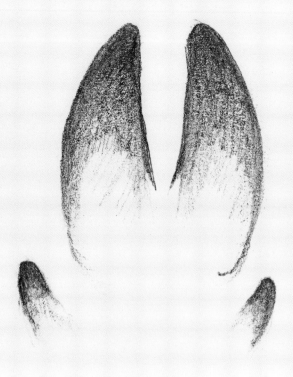

Front right print of adult male (actual size)

pellets. These form a clump of dung, which remains intact or breaks a little as it hits the floor.

OTHER SIGN

Wild boar are important architects of change in natural landscapes. Their rooting behaviour creates areas of disturbed ground, which in turn encourages the growth of annual wildflowers, such as poppies and cornflowers. Where boar have been foraging for subterranean foodstuffs, like tubers, roots and grubs, they can shift an astonishing amount of earth. Their nose and jaws are tough and able to dig into even frozen ground, and their neck muscles are immensely strong, creating a living plough. They lift whole turfs and turn them over to allow access to the ground beneath, and this activity can be spread over a wide area. This is especially true if a group of females and their young is feeding together.

Male boar scent mark trees, branches and other features in their territory, especially during the rut in

the autumn, but also at other times of year. They make gouges in the trunks of trees too, when they drag their sharp tusks across the bark. These gouges are often deep and look as though they may have been made by a sharp knife.

Like all members of the pig family, boar like to wallow and well-used wallows have clear footprints around their border, identifying their owners. Nearby trees are used as rubbing posts and will have large amounts of earth smeared on their lower trunk.

HOME

Boar do not make dens as such, but a farrowing sow creates a makeshift nest around her when she gives birth and is suckling very small piglets. These nests are often under the cover of thick vegetation, such as bramble thickets, and comprise grasses and dead leaves piled up and around her body. She may pay particular attention to extra cover on the north side of the nest in regions with northerly winds that could chill small young.

[ABOVE LEFT] Adult male wild boar are large, powerful animals, capable of moving a tremendous amount of earth in a single night while foraging.

[ABOVE RIGHT] Sheets of turf that have been lifted and turned almost intact are the work of boar.

[ABOVE] Hair may be snagged on wire fences where boar push through. Piglets have bi-coloured hair with orange and black bands.

WILD BOAR SENSES

Sound	Sight	Smell
8	7	10

WILD BOAR'S YEAR

Mating: September–November in UK

Gestation: 115–140 days (longer in older sows)

Young: litter of 4–6 piglets born February–May

HOW TO WATCH

Wild boar became extinct in the UK towards the end of the 13th century. There were several attempts to reintroduce them as a hunting resource, but it is generally accepted that there were no wild boar free ranging in Britain from the end of the 16th century.

Recent escapes from farmed populations have led to wild boar becoming re-established in the wild in many parts of the British Isles, with particularly viable populations in the Forest of Dean and in the Weald in Kent and Sussex.

They are largely crepuscular and nocturnal, though in areas of low disturbance they may be active by day, especially sounders of several females with young.

Wild boar can be wary or relatively confiding, depending on their previous experiences with humans. My contact with free-ranging wild boar in the UK has all been in the Forest of Dean where there are forestry enclosures that show significant sign of boar and areas where they regularly feed. A quiet vigil in such places, either sitting with minimal cover or in the shelter of a field hide (page 24), can yield fabulous views.

You may well encounter signs of activity by the roadside, where the boar have rooted up vast tracts of vegetation, but observation of the animals in this situation is difficult and potentially dangerous for both boar and observer.

In continental Europe, I have watched boar in forest and field environments. On a number of occasions I have reacted to hearing their contact calls and stalked close to them, paying careful attention to the wind direction and keeping all movement to an absolute minimum before settling into a good observation point. In the forests of Holland I have had great views of wild boar from purpose-built wooden hides set up close to forest clearings.

[RIGHT] Adult boar hair is very coarse, dark over its entire length and the tips are often split and frayed.

MICE AND VOLES

The following rodents – the house mouse (*Mus musculus*), wood mouse (*Apodemus sylvaticus*), yellow-necked mouse (*Apodemus flavicollis*), field vole (*Microtus agrestis*) and bank vole (*Myodes glareolus*) – do not generally lend themselves to protracted field observation in any but a few very specific situations.

The most reliable method of encounter is to establish a small mammal feeding station, described on page 125.

All five species featured here remain active throughout the year, and numbers generally peak towards the end of summer and are at their lowest in the early spring before the first litters are born.

SIGN
FOOTPRINTS

Prints show four toes on the forefoot, five on the hind. The tracks of this group of animals are so similar as to be inseparable in normal field conditions. There are slight differences in size between the species, the largest being the yellow-necked mouse and the smallest the field vole and house mouse, but there is such overlap between different age groups and genders as to render any tracks irrelevant in the field.

WOOD MOUSE
Weight: 13–27g
Length to rump: 81–103mm
Tail length: 71–95mm

FIELD VOLE
Weight: 20–40g
Length to rump: 90–115mm
Tail length: 30–50mm

Wood mouse prints (actual size)
Rear foot (left); front foot (right)

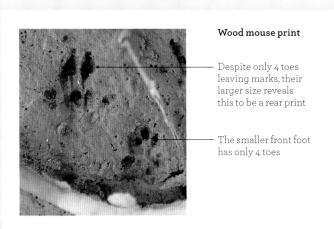

Wood mouse print

Despite only 4 toes leaving marks, their larger size reveals this to be a rear print

The smaller front foot has only 4 toes

On very rare occasions, field voles leave tracks on soft, finely grained soil. Note the four-toed prints from the front feet, and the five toes on the rear feet.

[ABOVE LEFT] Wood mice are largely nocturnal, as is reflected by their big, light-gathering eyes.

[ABOVE RIGHT] Field voles have relatively small eyes and are mostly active by day.

All these creatures are so light that tracks are only made naturally in the very rare conditions of fine grain soils and clays with just the right moisture content.

FAECES *Droppings*

The droppings of these animals are broadly similar – small (2-4mm), cylindrical and tapered at each end. Voles have more uniformly shaped droppings than mice. They also create latrines or middens in runs that are part of their access network in vegetation, often near the base of long grass. The summer droppings of field voles are greenish, due to their fresh grass diet, but in winter they tend to be blackish or brown because of drier foodstuffs. All other species tend to produce black or very dark faeces.

The mice tend to deposit their droppings widely as they move through any habitat. When this is in a man-made environment, such as a house or outbuilding, collections of droppings may be found where the mice settle to rest or feed. Wood and yellow-necked mouse droppings are virtually identical, with irregular outer edges and often a fibrous texture, though this depends on diet. House mice produce smaller droppings which are almost invariably very dark brown or black. Another distinguishing feature of house mouse droppings and urine is their scent which, unlike that of its more rural cousins, is quite pungent and musky. Urine trails are left as house mice move through their environment and the scent from these may build up over time so as to become overwhelming to the human nose. These urine trails leave dark, slightly oily-looking trails at points of high traffic.

FOOD REMAINS

What their footprints and droppings lack in individuality, mice and voles make up for in the way they gnaw their food. All are partial to the kernels of hazelnuts and a careful examination of the toothmarks made in the shells of a nut that has been eaten can tell you a great deal about which species ate it.

Essentially, mice and voles tackle hazelnuts with different techniques. The wood mouse holds the nut in its forefeet and gets a purchase on the outer edge of the nut with its upper incisors. It then brings its lower incisors across the shell in a rasping action. This is repeated as the mouse slowly turns the nut until it has drilled an access hole. The mouse then enlarges this and removes the kernel with its lower incisors. A distinctive ring of notches made by the upper incisors is left on the outside upper edge of the shell, while the gnawed face of the nut has regular grooves, made by the lower incisors, which run perpendicular to the outer edge.

Conversely, a field vole uses its upper incisors to drill into the nutshell, again turning the nut in its forefeet. When access has been gained, the vole feeds by scraping into the kernel with its upper incisors. Few or no marks are left on the upper outside edge of the shell, but the gnawed face of the nut will show grooves running perpendicular to the outer edge, similar to the marks left by wood mice. The inner surface may have a row of notches a millimetre or so below

Field voles create dropping middens at strategic points along their runs. These are usually shielded from view by a cover of long grass. Summer droppings have a greenish hue due to the fresh grass diet. Winter droppings are darker and coarser because the voles are eating drier grass.

Hazelnuts eaten by a bank vole [TOP] and a wood mouse [ABOVE]. Note the lack of toothmarks on the outer edge of the nut eaten by the vole.

the rim, created as the vole's upper incisors hit the edge when scraping out the kernel.

For comparison, see the pictures of nuts eaten by dormouse (page 129) and squirrel (page 137).

Similar marks are made on sloe pips and cherry stones, though due to the smaller nature of these nuts, voles may leave some notches on the outer upper edge, making it very tricky to differentiate between those taken by voles and those taken by mice.

Mice tend to carry nuts to a safe feeding place, or even a hoarding pile under the cover of a log or rock, and these may be discovered by turning over such features.

Mice feed on pine seeds, chewing away the scales of the cone to reach the nutritious seeds within. Chewed cones tend to have very rounded bases and may be chewed all the way to the top, leaving a handful of scales at the tip which do not bear seeds. A litter of scales is likely to be found all around the immediate vicinity of a cone eaten in this way, and the base of each is gnawed evenly. Compare this with squirrel sign (page 137).

HOME

Wood mice and yellow-necked mice both excavate extensive burrow systems, using their forefeet to dig and their hind feet to push back soil. Wood mice, especially, may create complex systems of multiple chambers, with resting and natal chambers lined with fine grasses and dry leaves. In winter, several mice may huddle together in the same nest, but during spring and summer more territorial behaviour leads to greater dispersal of adults. Mouse holes and chambers are an important resource for nesting bumble bees, some species of which build their own nests in abandoned mouse nests. Both mouse species use existing crannies and chambers in drystone walls and other man-made structures.

House mice may be almost exclusively associated with human habitation in some parts of their range, occupying cavities in walls, beneath floors and any other cover where they can find sanctuary with access to food within the building. Elsewhere they are common in agricultural landscapes, though the numbers living in arable fields

have dropped massively with the introduction of mechanised grain harvesting.

Both bank and field voles are active burrowers, though bank voles tend to make more extensive subterranean networks than their cousins, with chambers below the earth surface. Field voles frequently nest under logs or other cover. Refugia (sheets of corrugated tin or the equivalent) are frequently adopted by field voles as resting and nesting sites and it is common to lift a tin sheet to be greeted by the beady eyes of a vole that was hiding beneath it.

Field voles make extensive runs in suitable habitat, which criss-cross mature grassland at ground level. They maintain regular peep-holes around the network, which appear as small rounded holes in the otherwise tangled sward. Field vole feeding sites are distinctive, with tightly nibbled grasses and collections of brown or greenish droppings, often close to the site of a peep-hole. If snow covers the ground, field voles will try to keep their peep-holes open

[ABOVE LEFT] Good field vole habitat includes plenty of long, rank grasses ideally forming a thatch from the previous year's growth. Small holes in the thatch betray the presence of voles.

[ABOVE RIGHT] By gently peeling back the thatch from around a peep-hole, you can reveal the multiple runs made by the voles. Replace the thatch once you have had a look.

MOUSE AND VOLE SENSES

Sound	Sight	Smell
6	3	2

to the air, and in areas of high vole population the snow will be peppered with many small holes, 2–3cm across, evenly spaced around the covered grassland.

None of these rodents hibernates and all have multiple litters of young throughout their extensive breeding season, which usually runs from March to October. House mice may breed at any time of year in the sheltered environment of a human dwelling.

HOW TO WATCH

Watching any of these species in the field is challenging, due to their nervous disposition and often nocturnal habits. Voles tend to be more active by day than mice, though both can be seen during daylight hours.

An established feeding station can provide excellent views of all species. If suitable food (grain, nuts and fruit with some mealworms) is placed on the ground near cover, such as dense vegetation or a log pile or drystone wall, it will be visited. A rather more elaborate feeding station can be established for very close observation by building a box with an open side pushed tight against a window behind which the observer sits. Low-intensity lighting can be introduced to the box and access to it should be through holes or tunnels of 3–4cm in diameter (larger holes will allow access to the more dominant brown rat). Similar feed placed inside the box will encourage visits from any or all of the species described above.

None of these species sees inanimate forms very well but all react swiftly to movement. If you are in a position to watch at very close quarters, keep as still as possible.

HARVEST MOUSE *Micromys minutus*

This is the smallest British mammal, and the only one with a prehensile tail.

It spends most of its life climbing through vegetation or resting in nests made of fine grasses. Some of these nests are tucked into the base of plants but many are built above ground level, suspended in more robust stems.

It is rare indeed to spot harvest mice in the wild and, apart from their nests, they leave little or no sign. Droppings are minute and since the mice rarely come down to the ground the chances of finding a footprint are virtually nil.

In suitable habitat, though, it is sometimes possible to watch harvest mice, especially at dawn and dusk. If you find what you think may be a harvest mouse nest, keep a silent vigil from a distance of a few metres and you may be lucky enough to spot these tiny acrobats clambering through plant stems in search of seeds and small invertebrates.

SIZE
Weight: 4–6g
Length to rump: 50–70mm
Tail length: 45mm

Harvest mice use their prehensile tails as a fifth limb, clambering through vegetation to reach the seeds, bugs and berries that make up their diet.

DORMOUSE *Muscardinus avellanarius*

SIGN
FOOTPRINTS
Dormice spend almost their entire lives climbing through scrub, grasses and trees, so finding a footprint is extremely unlikely. The hind footprint can be told apart from that of other small rodents because the fifth vestigial digit has no claw. The forefoot is longer than it is wide (unlike that of most other small rodents) and has four long toes with small claw marks. The hind footprint is 1.5cm long by 1.1cm wide. The forefoot print measures 1cm long by 80mm wide.

SIZE
Weight: 15–25g
Length to rump: 80mm
Tail length: 65mm

FAECES *Droppings*
You are most unlikely to find dormouse droppings, since they are deposited randomly as the animal climbs through its leafy world. They closely resemble the droppings of a field vole (page 122).

FOOD REMAINS
Dormice feed on a wide variety of seeds, fruits, pollen and insects. Many meals leave no sign and only when they eat hazelnuts do they leave characteristic feeding signs.

The dormouse holds the nut between its forefeet, then gnaws across the top diagonally. The result is a clean, almost polished-looking gnawed surface with faint oblique tooth marks. Compare this to the work of mice and voles, which leave tooth marks that run perpendicular to the outer edge of the shell (page 123).

OTHER SIGN
Dormice build nests from a mixture of vegetation, but where honeysuckle is available, they use strips of the bark to build their dome-shaped retreats. Bark is usually removed mid-height in the shrub layer and is taken in long, thin strips.

HOME
Dormice build their nests anywhere from a few centimetres above ground to high up in the branches of a tree. Most are in the shrub layer. Free-standing nests are made of many

DORMOUSE SENSES

Sound | Sight | Smell
7 | 5 | 3

DORMOUSE'S YEAR

Hibernation: October–April

Mating: from early May

Gestation: 22–24 days

Young: 2–4 litters of up to 9 young born from late May

Hazelnuts eaten by a dormouse. The nuts have been gnawed obliquely, resulting in a polished inner rim, with few obvious toothmarks. The outer edge of the rim has many marks made by the dormouse's lower incisors, which are used to get a purchase on the nut while the upper incisors scrape through the shell.

strips of thin bark, usually honeysuckle, woven together into a ball-shaped mass that is about 15cm across. The entrance hole is often very obscure.

Dormice readily take to nest boxes intended for members of the tit family, or boxes erected specially for them. The latter have an entrance hole of about 3cm diameter which faces the trunk of the tree or shrub they are mounted on. Access is made possible by wooden spacers which hold the box a couple of centimetres away from the tree. The dormouse is protected by law, and its nests can only be inspected under licence.

HOW TO WATCH

This is a wholly nocturnal species and very difficult to watch in the wild. Thermal-imaging equipment can pinpoint dormice as they climb through the scrub and tree canopy. Other night-viewing equipment (IR or image intensifiers) only has value in areas where dormice are known to exist and where day roosts are known as a starting point for observations at dusk.

Dormice in captivity (observed under licence) tend to remain immobile for long periods unless there is some background white noise, such as the sound of a fan blowing on to dead leaves or a radio broadcasting static. The reason for this is unknown, though it seems likely that dormice are nervous of creating sounds in an otherwise silent environment as they move though the leaf canopy, since this may draw the attention of predators such as owls.

Sleeping dormice can only be checked in nest boxes by licensed handlers. The little animals tend to go into torpor if the temperature is low (below 17°C) and do not wake immediately, even when a nesting box has been opened, making it easy to inspect them.

WATER VOLE *Arvicola amphibius*

SIGN
FOOTPRINTS
The water vole's hind foot is marginally larger than its forefoot, measuring about 2.7cm wide compared to 2.5cm. Prints show four toes on the forefoot, five on the hind, and the hind footprint often slightly overlaps the heel of the forefoot in the normal track pattern. The overall impression is of a well-splayed, star-shaped print from both fore and hind feet, with the outer toes often diametrically opposed to each other.

Because of the water vole's wetland habitat, prints are commonly found in wet mud bordering lakes, rivers and streams. Be mindful that brown rats inhabit this same habitat and their tracks are very similar to those of a water vole, though marginally less well splayed for the most part.

FAECES *Droppings*
Water voles create middens on emergent rocks, logs or other objects within their watery world. There may be collections of droppings on small plateaus on the river bank and on wooden structures close to the water's surface, as are sometimes found on the edges of bridges. The droppings

SIZE
Male slightly larger than female
Weight: about 300g
Length to rump: about 18cm
Tail length: about 11cm

Front right print (actual size)

Rear right print (actual size)

Four toes on front foot
Toes spread wide

Five toes on rear foot
Toes spread wide

Rear footprint often
oversteps front print

[ABOVE LEFT] Burrows are usually close to the water's edge and near deeper water. Some entrances may be below the surface, especially on river banks where water levels vary greatly.

[ABOVE RIGHT] Water voles are best watched during the summer months, when activity outside the burrow is more common.

[OPPOSITE] Latrines are stationed on bankside ledges near nest entrances and floating vegetation. Middens of greenish-brown droppings, about 1cm long, are used by voles as scented territory markers.

are typical of a vole, though larger than those of any other vole species in the region. Brown rat droppings, which are similar, tend to be black or brown and coarser in texture. Rat latrines are usually away from the water's edge and never on floating vegetation or branches.

The colour of the droppings varies from greenish during the summer months, due to a diet of fresh grasses and other vegetation, to brown in the winter when the voles change to dried food sources.

FOOD REMAINS

Nibbled vegetation in the immediate vicinity of burrow entrance holes is common. Where there is a seasonal glut of a plant species, water voles may drag leaves and stalks back to the entrance burrow, both to store within the burrow and to feed upon close to the entrance. In winter, they may gnaw tree roots, and sometimes nibble away the bark of small trees, especially young ash, to gain access to the sugar-rich cambium. This feeding behaviour leaves distinctive shards of bark, rounded along one edge, littering the floor beneath the tree. Water voles are poor climbers and can only reach up the tree as far as they can stretch from the ground – about 20cm.

HOME

This species digs extensive burrow systems usually, but not always, along the banks of freshwater systems. Burrow entrances may be along the top of the bank, at or near water level, and some may be below the water's surface. Hole entrances measure 6–8cm in diameter. Where earth is excavated on top of a bank, piles of discarded soil are pushed to one side of the burrow entrance. These 'hills' superficially resemble molehills, but they are not as uniform in shape and the burrow entrance is visible to one side of the mound. Vegetation is usually nibbled short, close to the hole entrance. This habit of moving the spoil heap away distinguishes the digging habits of this species from those of brown rats, which leave fan-shaped spoil heaps emanating from the entrance to their burrows.

Nests are usually built deep within the burrow system, but in some marshland habitats, large balls (about the size of a football) of dried grasses and other vegetation may be found wound into the tangle of emergent marsh plants. Water voles do not hibernate but in colder regions they may stay in their burrow system through the winter.

HOW TO WATCH

Water voles are active day and night, and cycles of activity take place every two to four hours. Where brown rats occupy the same habitat, water voles are likely to be more active in daylight so as not to compete with the more nocturnal rats.

They react negatively to physical changes in their known environment so care must be taken not to disturb bankside vegetation or other features in order to get a clearer view of a midden or feeding area. Water vole vision is acutely sensitive to movement, so a patient sit-and-wait strategy can be effective as long as no movement whatsoever is made by the observer. Exceptions to this can be seen where a population of voles is exposed to repeated benign contact with humans, such as publicly accessed ponds and lakes.

Water voles can be tempted to feed in the open with the introduction of attractive foods, especially apple pieces and blackberries. Feeding stations can be set up several days ahead of observation to maximise chances of an encounter.

WATER VOLE SENSES

Sound	Sight	Smell
6	**8**	**3**

WATER VOLE'S YEAR

Mating: from February

Gestation: 20–30 days

Young: up to 5 litters of up to 6 young born from late March

[ABOVE] A patient vigil in known water vole habitats will eventually give views of the animals emerging to feed or gather fresh vegetation.

BROWN RAT *Rattus norvegicus*

SIGN
FOOTPRINT
Brown rat prints are sometimes found in the soft mud margins of rivers and ponds or on other soft substrate after rain. Forefeet have four well-splayed toes and hind feet have five. Claw marks show at the tip of each. The hind foot measures 2.1cm long by 2cm wide and the forefoot 1.5cm long by 1.7cm wide.

FAECES *Droppings*
Droppings measure 11mm long by 4mm wide and are cylindrical and rounded at both ends. They vary in colour, depending on the diet of the rat. The texture is rather coarse and fibrous, though this also varies depending on the composition of recent meals.

Rats deposit their droppings in latrine sites, and clusters may be found under cover at points along well-used trails. They also deposit droppings randomly as they wander through their home ground. An adult will excrete about 40 droppings each day.

SIZE
Weight: 500g
Length to rump: 28cm
Tail length: 26cm

Front right print (actual size)

Rear right print (actual size)

Toes on both front and rear feet are not spread quite as wide as those on a water vole

Larger, five-toed rear foot often oversteps the smaller four-toed front foot

Droppings are left in loose clusters in latrine sites and singly along trails. Males deposit heavily scented urine around their territory.

OTHER SIGN

Urine is used as a scent trail, especially by male rats, and well-used paths and tracks that are under cover, especially those in man-made structures, develop staining from this and from the repeated passing of rat bodies. A distinctive musky scent is associated with these urine trails, not a smell I find attractive!

Rats can gain access to food or shelter by gnawing through wood, plasterboard, plastic and even soft metals. Gnaw sign bears the heavy, broad marks made by upper and lower incisors, each 'scallop' being 2mm or so wide. They are accomplished excavators and can dig through significant depths of soil or rubble to extend a burrow system or access a resource.

FOOD REMAINS

Rats can gnaw through remarkably tough materials and eat almost anything, animal or vegetable, they can get their teeth into.

Gnaw marks are broader than those made by mice or voles and rarely follow a consistent pattern on a nut shell or the equivalent. Instead a rat breaks into the kernel in whatever way it can. Piles of snail shells under a log or other low cover which have been broken into near their natural opening and chiselled away along the coil to access the soft body of the animal within, are a sign that a rat has been taking its mollusc prey there to eat undisturbed. Cereal grains are often nibbled at one end, the other end being discarded with obvious bite marks across their width. Rats will target pignut tubers (*Conopodium majus*), and leave

BROWN RAT SENSES

Sound	Sight	Smell
9	**3**	**7**

BROWN RAT'S YEAR

Mating: any time of year in suitable conditions, though usually February–October

Gestation: 21–24 days

Young: up to 5 litters of 7–8 young born each year, usually March–November

[OPPOSITE] Brown rats thrive almost anywhere, not least around human habitation, where they make the most of our food waste.

characteristic conical snuff holes where they have dug and forced their faces into the soil, sometimes leaving traces of the gnawed tuber still in the ground. They may also target the eggs and nestlingsof ground-nesting birds.

HOME

Rats build nests anywhere that is dry, secure and relatively warm. They can be in natural cavities, the disused burrows of other animals or man-made structures. They are also very accomplished excavators and dig extensive burrow systems and chambers. Where rats have access to a prolific food source, they may coexist in very large numbers, but more natural colonies are modest in size, with family groups occupying a burrow system.

Rat holes are about 7cm across and rounded. Spoil heaps outside the tunnel entrance may be large, but do not contain bedding material. There are rarely droppings on the spoil heaps. Regularly used rat runs show smooth wear due to the constant passage of feet and low-slung bodies.

HOW TO WATCH

Rats are largely nocturnal unless undisturbed or under pressure to find enough food – for example, in the winter months in rural areas. A percentage of large populations will also venture out by day to avoid competition. Rats have excellent hearing, a great sense of smell and react adversely to movement, though their eyesight is their weakest sense.

Dusk is typically the best time to watch brown rats in visible light and a simple sit-and-wait method in suitable habitat will yield results. Rats readily visit feeding stations and are often quick to discover food put out for birds, taking anything that has dropped to the ground and learning to access the food in hanging feeders.

They are neophobic, reacting adversely to anything new placed in their environment, so care must be taken not to change any element of the site before observations start. They also react negatively to torchlight shone on them, and seem just as aware of red light as they are white light. Infrared light does not seem to affect them so hand-held IR night-viewing equipment (page 9) can be used.

RED SQUIRREL *Sciurus vulgaris*

SIGN

FOOTPRINTS

The chances of finding a squirrel footprint are very slight.
When squirrels do come down to the forest floor, the ground
litter of dead leaves or pine needles means that they leave
no mark as they walk. On the rare occasions when they trot
over mud soft enough to bear their print, or run over snow-
covered ground, they do so with a bounding gait, leaving
gaps of about 50cm between sets. Forefeet show four widely
spaced toes with very fine claw marks in front of each, and
four very closely aligned pads on the palm. Hind feet have
five toes, again with claws showing, and four closely aligned
plantar pads. On very soft ground there may be a small
mark left by the metatarsal pad.

SIZE
Male is slightly larger than female
Weight: about 300g
Length to rump: about 22cm
Tail length: about 18cm

FAECES *Droppings*

Squirrels allow their droppings to fall randomly as they
make their way through the trees and it is very unlikely you
will find any collection of their faeces. Each is about 6mm
long and looks a little like a small roe deer dropping – almost
spherical or bean shaped, with a small nipple at one end
and a dimple at the other. Close inspection of the contents
reveals vegetable matter and occasionally insect remains.
You are unlikely to find any sign of squirrel droppings in
summer, but in winter, if snow lies on the ground beneath

**Front right print
(actual size)**   **Rear right print
(actual size)**

Rear foot, with five
widely spaced toes

Heel pad may leave
elongated mark when
squirrel sits up

[TOP] A squirrel splits a hazelnut neatly down the centre with a single bite, leaving two half shells with few or no toothmarks.

[ABOVE] Squirrels chew each scale from a pine cone to access the seeds. Bites on scale roots tend to move around the cone in one direction, leaving a neat edge on one side of the bite and a ragged tear on the other.

trees, small discoloured holes in the snow may reveal where a dropping has fallen through from a height.

FOOD REMAINS

Almost wherever squirrels feed and whatever they feed upon, they leave distinctive sign.

When eating hazelnuts, a squirrel holds the nut in its forepaws and applies pressure top and bottom with its upper and lower incisors to open it. Experienced squirrels find the weak seam of a nut easily and manage a clean break, neatly cracking the nut down the middle into two halves that they let fall to the floor. Younger squirrels may not be as adept, and chew at the nut before cracking it open to get to the kernel. Crucially, at least some of the nut will have been opened by the exertion of pressure and there will be a portion that has cracked open along a weak fault in the shell.

Squirrels access pine seeds by chewing away the scales of a cone, leaving the core, or axis, naked but for the few scales at the tip. These are left intact, in part because the squirrel uses its forepaw to secure the cone by them, and also because they rarely harbour good seeds to eat. Soft scales are torn off with ease, but tougher scales have to be chewed off one by one. The bottom of each cone reveals the squirrel's method of working, either right- or left-handed. A right-handed squirrel holds the cone with the bottom to the left and the tip to the right. It starts work from the bottom up, holding the cone down firmly. It executes each bite across the cone, leaving sheared scale bases attached to the axis, with a short edge where the bite started furthest from the squirrel and a longer edge where it was finished. Left-handed squirrels leave the opposite pattern as the cone is rotated and seeds consumed. The base scales of most cones are completely removed, leaving a tattered-looking bottom.

Compare this to a cone that has been eaten by a mouse or vole, neither of which is powerful enough to tear off the base scales and so have to chew each one away, leaving a neat, rounded base.

Squirrels may from time to time feed on the nutrient-rich phloem and cambium beneath tree bark, especially in the months from May through to July, when the sap is running. This can lead to extensive damage to the tree and, in

exceptional cases, to its death above the gnaw line. Areas of stripped bark, sometimes in a spiral pattern, high up among the branches are the work of squirrels and closer inspection reveals clear tooth marks.

OTHER SIGN
Squirrels cache food in response to any glut. This is usually done on the ground, with each item being buried in a shallow pit, then covered with soil and leaf litter. Caches appear to be sniffed out rather than remembered, but the general area of caches may be recalled. When they remove items from these stores, squirrels leave small snuff holes, often with an arch of vegetation or soil, where they have pushed their muzzle into the ground to retrieve the item.

HOME *Drey*
Dreys may be built within tree cavities and large nest boxes or can be free standing among the branches of trees, usually close to the trunk. The latter are made of a mix of twigs, stripped bark, mosses and leaves

[OPPOSITE] Food remains are often found on the top of logs or tree stumps, where squirrels sit to keep an eye out for danger while feeding.

RED SQUIRREL SENSES

Sound	Sight	Smell
7	9	3

RED SQUIRREL'S YEAR

Hibernation: does not hibernate, but in colder regions may become less active in winter, eating stored food to survive

Mating: from January

Gestation: 38–39 days

Young: up to 2 litters of up to 6 young born from mid-February

and look like rounded, football-sized bundles of vegetation. The entrance is on one side and may be filled in during cold weather or if a female squirrel leaves a nursery drey for a period of time.

HOW TO WATCH

Red squirrels are active by day, though they may wake well before sunrise and return to the sleeping drey at last light. Populations vary hugely in their response to human presence, depending on their experiences of contact. In some areas they happily take food from the hand; in others, they beat a hasty retreat at the first sign of a human in their midst.

For good protracted views, establish a feeding station. Choose a tree stump or other feature that will afford the animal good all-round views as it feeds, and bait it with unsalted peanuts or other attractive seeds or pulses. Introduce a portable hide to the scene and continue baiting for a week or so before considering a vigil. On the day of observation, arrive before first light and bait the log, then retire to the hide. With good fortune you will be graced with superb views of feeding squirrels.

For a more natural approach, a careful sit-and-wait method in suitable habitat usually works better than actively trying to track squirrels through woodland. If they feel they are being followed they are likely to disappear and can very easily shake off a human observer if they choose to. Even where red squirrels are used to close contact with humans, they are neophobic and will often react adversely to new elements introduced to a well-practised regime. If, for example, a squirrel regularly visits a feeding station, a person sitting close to that place will dissuade the animal from visiting. Every new element must be introduced carefully and slowly for successful observation.

Squirrels may draw attention to themselves with vocalisations. Mating chases are often accompanied by 'chucking' calls and, if a squirrel spots a danger, such as a roosting owl, it will call repeatedly from a safe vantage point. Mimicry of these calls may draw a curious squirrel a little closer, but is of little value for protracted observation.

GREY SQUIRREL *Sciurus carolinensis*

SIGN

FOOTPRINTS

Prints are identical to the prints of a red squirrel (page 136), but they are slightly larger. Both species tend to bound when on the ground and forefoot tracks are left behind the hind foot tracks.

See red squirrel for other details of sign, from which the grey squirrel is virtually indistinguishable.

SIZE
Male slightly larger than female
Weight: 400–600g
Length to rump: 23–30cm
Tail length: 19–25cm

Rear right print (actual size)

Squirrels may rest and nest in cavities in trees, or build a drey [ABOVE] from twigs, strips of bark and dry leaves.

BEAVER *Castor fiber*

SIGN

FOOTPRINTS

The beaver leaves a large, broad hind footprint with
a long heel and five long, forward-facing toes (the fifth
inside toe often doesn't register deeply). In soft mud,
webbing between the toes leaves an imprint. The front
print is much smaller than the hind and often partly
obliterated by the hind foot. It has five splayed toes
but again, often only four register in the print.

FAECES *Scat*

Beavers defecate in the water, so the chances
of finding any scat on land are very remote.
Each scat is full of fibrous vegetation remains
and quickly breaks up and disintegrates after
it has been excreted.

FOOD REMAINS

Food and dam building go hand in hand with
beavers and their legendary industry is borne out
by reality. Where beavers enter a wetland system,
they soon begin a process of felling bankside
trees and using the timber to build their dams.
A beaver-felled tree is unmistakable, bearing the
deep gouges and scallops created by the beaver's
powerful gnawing; a pointed stump surrounded
by wood shavings remains. Sheared rushes
and other green materials are typical signs
of feeding on vegetation.

OTHER SIGN

Trails to and from water may be heavily worn
by repeated passage of the animals and dragging
of timber to build dams and lodges.

SIZE
Weight: 16–30kg
Length to rump: 60–90cm
Tail length: 20–35cm

Front and rear right prints (actual size)
Front foot often overstepped by large rear foot

HOME

In some environments beavers may build lodges comprising vast piles of logs. Elsewhere, they may dig burrows in suitable soil alongside water.

HOW TO WATCH

Beavers are crepuscular and nocturnal, so the best views are likely to be had at dusk and dawn.

They can be very wary or relatively confiding, depending on their previous experiences with human contact. In Britain, persecution drove beavers to extinction in the 16th century, but the species has recently been successfully reintroduced to both Scotland and southern England.

Once a location has been established through sign, a quiet vigil at dusk, watching the water body closest to the freshest signs of gnawing or dam building is usually successful. Aim to arrive at the location with at least an hour to go before sunset, preferably longer. Settle into a bankside vantage point with your outline obscured and the wind blowing your scent away from the water. Listen for loud, solid sounding water movement and watch for ripples emanating from the bank. A relaxed beaver is likely to swim out on the surface, but may swim beneath the surface as it emerges. Watch the water for surface ripples created by the swimming action of the animal as it thrusts with its hind feet and tail. These 'footprints' on the surface reveal the sub-aquatic progress of a swimming animal, though they often disappear into bankside vegetation before the beaver surfaces for air.

Deploy sit-and-wait tactics and be very careful with movement should a beaver on the surface be facing in your direction. They pick up on any movement very swiftly and quickly dive and disappear from view if they feel in the least bit threatened.

Feeding areas may be watched in a similar manner. Beavers feel secure when they are close to their aquatic escape route, so virtually all activity takes place within a few metres of the water's edge, or in the water itself.

BEAVER SENSES

Sound	Sight	Smell
8	8	3

BEAVER'S YEAR

Mating: January/February

Gestation: 105 days

Young: 1 litter of 2–3 kits born in April–June; emerge with parents in June/July

[OPPOSITE TOP LEFT] The work of beavers on trees close to water is unmistakable. These animals are important architects in our landscape, creating habitat opportunities for many creatures and helping to keep water clean.

[OPPOSITE TOP RIGHT] Dams are built along waterways, managing water flow and making pools which are used by the beavers and myriad other animals.

[OPPOSITE BOTTOM] Beavers tend to be most active at dusk and dawn. Where they are undisturbed, they forage and socialise in broad daylight.

RABBIT *Oryctolagus cuniculus*

SIGN
FOOTPRINTS

In common with brown hares, rabbits usually move through grassland or other vegetation, and you rarely come across their footprints under these conditions. Unlike hares, however, rabbits commonly set up home in sand dunes and here you can often find their tracks. In normal bounding gait, rabbits leave two small, teardrop-shaped indents in the sand with their forefeet, one in front of the other and just out of line with each other. The large hind feet leave elongated prints in the sand, alongside or just in front of the leading forefoot. When a rabbit stops to browse or scent mark, the full length of the hind feet may leave parallel depressions in the sand.

Rabbits rarely travel far along traditional paths (unlike badgers, for example) but do repeatedly use the same access points in and out of fields and into favoured feeding areas. These runs tend to be most noticeable through hedges and under fences and may well form a broken line where the animals regularly hop to or from a field. These hopping tracks may be worn smooth, each bare patch being roughly 30cm apart.

FAECES *Droppings*

These are arguably one of the most familiar of all wild animal signs, thanks largely to our habit of keeping rabbits in captivity. Wild rabbit droppings are about 1cm in diameter and roughly spherical. They vary in colour depending on the animal's diet, which varies from location to location and by season. Most are dark brown when fresh, drying to a greenish-brown over time.

Rabbits frequently create large latrines, with hundreds of droppings littering the ground in one spot, often on a tussock or raised patch of ground. These serve as smelly territorial markers for a

SIZE
Weight: 1.2– 2kg
Length to rump: 40cm

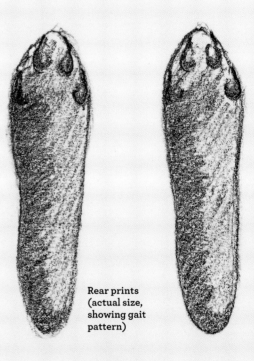

Rear prints (actual size, showing gait pattern)

Front prints (actual size)

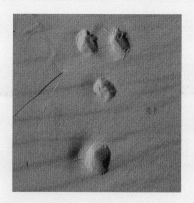

Prints in sand dunes can be distinct. Rear prints are almost always in parallel, while front prints are staggered and lie behind the rear.

community and may be used for generations. The effect on the vegetation on and around these latrines may be marked, with the extra nitrogen from the droppings encouraging the growth of many plants, especially nettles.

FOOD REMAINS

Most rabbit feeding sign is ambiguous, though a closely cropped area of grass close to a warren system is typical. As any forester or gardener knows, rabbits can and will eat virtually any vegetation and they have a habit of cropping favoured foods close to the ground.

Rabbits often scrape away at the ground with their forefeet to reach roots and tubers, and the little fan-shaped digs are very distinctive. They usually measure 5–6cm in length and 3–4cm at the widest point.

HAIR

Rabbit hair varies in colour depending on the part of the body it originates from – white from the underside, grey-brown from the upper body. Close inspection of individual upper body hairs reveals a grey base fading to beige, followed by a dark band and ending with a beige tip.

You rarely find rabbit hair snagged on barbed wire or brambles, but where animals have been fighting or attacked by a predator, clumps of hair may litter the ground.

HOME

Rabbits are excellent diggers, excavating large underground networks known as warrens. Entrance holes are rarely bigger than 30cm across and often smaller. The presence of copious droppings, grazed areas close by and the lack of distinct piles of bedding or clear claw marks in the soil of the spoil heaps all point to the work of this species. As with the rabbit's latrines, areas around well-used warrens often host stands of nettles and elder, both of which thrive on the extra nitrogen provided by the droppings.

Unlike young hares, rabbit young are altricial – that is, born blind, hairless and immobile. Breeding stops are blind burrows, often dug a little way away from the main warren. The doe plugs the breeding stop with bundles of grass when she is away from her young, and since she is only likely to

Rabbits create latrines or middens, with the whole community depositing their droppings in the same site. These act as scented territory markers.

visit her litter once a day to allow them to suckle, these breeding burrows are extremely difficult to spot.

Badgers sometimes locate breeding stops by scent. They dig out and consume the young rabbits, leaving a litter of dry grass and the fine hair from the mother's belly (which she uses in her breeding nest as bedding and insulation) strewn around the entrance (page 46). In any one year, fewer than ten per cent of young born are likely to survive into the following year. That said, rabbits are such prolific breeders, with four to seven litters of up to 12 young each in a year, that they now are estimated to number about 40 million animals in the UK alone.

HOW TO WATCH

In common with many wild mammals, rabbits behave differently towards humans depending on their life experience. In some areas of high human traffic and benign contact, rabbits can be incredibly confiding, especially when young. Some public parks and other publicly accessed areas have high wild rabbit populations that won't bat an eyelid at the approach of a human and may barely hop out of your path as you approach. Elsewhere, in areas (largely rural) where rabbits are persecuted, either through direct hunting

Warrens may be one or two holes or extensive networks of burrows, hosting large numbers of rabbits.

RABBIT'S YEAR

Mating: February–October

Gestation: 29–35 days

Young: 4–7 litters per year with an average 5 young born from late February onwards through the season

Young rabbits may be naive and much easier to observe than a wary adult.

RABBIT SENSES

Sound	Sight	Smell
8	8	3

[ABOVE] Adult rabbits are equipped with highly developed senses so attempting to get close to a nervous rabbit is a true test of your field skills.

or by dogs, they are hugely wary. With these more timid populations the use of a field or portable hide works well with all age groups. While you must be careful not to make a sound and keep all movement to a minimum, wind direction is less important since rabbits do not seem to respond negatively to human scent until it is very close to them – or perhaps they just can't smell us! It's hard to know which. That said, ensuring the wind is blowing from the rabbit to you means that any small sounds you may make are also less likely to reach their super-sensitive ears, so where possible take this precaution.

As a test of field skills and patience, I have sometimes made my way quietly to the centre of an active warren and made myself comfortable by lying prone on my belly, head on one side. After a while, young rabbits will begin to venture out of the warren and a little later adults may begin to emerge. As long as you remain perfectly still, most rabbits ignore your presence and may hop to within a metre or so of where you lie.

BROWN HARE *Lepus europaeus*

SIGN

FOOTPRINTS

Hares usually move through lush sward or other vegetation so one rarely comes across their footprints under normal conditions. When they do traverse sand, wet mud or snow with a bounding gait, they leave a distinctive pattern of prints with the two forefeet punching teardrop-shaped depressions, one before the other in a near linear track, and the large hind feet sitting alongside or just in front of the leading forefoot. A slow-moving hare travelling on deep snow or very wet mud may leave a long hind footprint showing the entire lower leg from the toes to the heel. More commonly, hares keep high on their hind feet and the track of the hind foot looks like that of a large cat, but with more pointed toes and visible claws.

FAECES *Droppings*

As you might expect, adult hare droppings look like super-sized rabbit droppings – rounded, sometimes with a slight point, and measuring 1.5–2cm in diameter. They frequently contain the remains of coarse grasses which are easy to see on the surface.

Unlike rabbit droppings, they are not deposited in middens but cast instead wherever the hare happens to be when it feels the urge. This may be close to a form, though rarely in one, since many of the droppings produced while a hare is resting are passed from the anus directly to the mouth to be re-digested. Small litters of droppings are sometimes found where a hare has been feeding.

FOOD REMAINS

A hare's diet is mostly made up of grasses and broad-leaved herbs like clover. They sometimes target the bark on the base of trees, especially during hard winter conditions when snowfall covers their preferred food. They leave distinctive toothmarks, with the upper incisors lodging a good grip on the tree while the lower incisors do most of the work stripping the bark. A tree attacked in this way will bear

SIZE

Weight: 2.5–7kg
Length to rump: 48–75cm
Length of tail: 7cm

Front right print (actual size)

Rear right print (actual size)

[TOP] Hares are well known for their showy displays of chasing and boxing in spring and summer. Males pursue females as the latter approach oestrus, but they are rebuffed if the female is not ready to mate, leading to boxing bouts.

[ABOVE] Droppings are scattered randomly as hares feed.

the telltale marks of a nibbling hare: the upper incisors each have a groove running down their centre and where they lodge to give the hare grip before gnawing, they leave four distinct marks, all very close together. Hares are big animals with remarkably long hind legs, and so can reach a long way up the trunk of a tree to feed. In deep snow their reach is, of course, even higher, assisted by the drifting.

Hares nibble the tops from young trees, though distinguishing this sign from that made by other creatures that feed in the same manner, such as rabbits or roe deer, is virtually impossible.

HAIR

Hare hair (I've always wanted to write that!) is reddish-brown with a darker base than tip, giving the animal a grizzled appearance in the field. You rarely come across it, unless a hare has been killed by a predator such as a fox or goshawk, and at such kill sites other body parts are likely to be present, making identification more straightforward.

HOME

Hares do not make a home as such, but when they rest, they simply hunker down in a patch of longer vegetation or a dip in the land and lie squat to the ground in a depression known as a form. They may on rare occasions scrape the ground to create a deeper depression than they can find naturally. Hare forms are usually very difficult to discern, but once you get your eye in you may be able to pick out the elongated, oval-shaped area of flattened vegetation made by the body of the animal. Hares may return to a favourite form if undisturbed and these may be easier to spot, especially in long vegetation with a bower of grasses forming over the place where the hare's back end rests.

Young hares, or leverets, are precocial: born above ground, fully furred with their eyes open and are able to hop within hours of birth. They, too, rest in forms during the day, the litter spread out singly over a wide area and only coming together to join their mother at dusk to suckle.

Between feeds from their mother (which only take place once a day) leverets lie alone, still and apparently abandoned. If you come across one, leave well alone unless you are completely certain that its mother has been killed.

HOW TO WATCH

Hares are visual creatures and while resting in their forms have a remarkable field of view without having to move a muscle. This is thanks to the position and protrusion of their eyes, high on their heads. The only blind spot is directly behind them at close proximity. Suffice it to say, not much gets past a hare!

If you spot a hare resting in its form at relatively close quarters, deploy the 'disinterested' observation technique (page 17) and it will almost certainly sit tight.

Hare behaviour is easiest to watch early in the season, when they are breeding. While breeding occurs throughout the summer, by mid-June in most habitats the vegetation grows too high to make hare watching easy. Notable exceptions to this are in the far north of the hare's range and in grassland or arable fields that have been grazed or recently cut. For the most part, hares are nocturnal creatures, stirring shortly before dusk, then heading out to feed throughout the night. When breeding, however, activity can occur throughout the day and this makes for great opportunities to watch them.

Always start a day's hare watching before sunrise to get an idea of where the animals are and where they may choose to rest through the day as they settle from their night's feeding. If there is little or no breeding activity, they are likely to be well spaced and moving as singles to their forms before settling to sleep. If, however, there is a female hare nearing oestrus, then the social dynamic changes considerably. She is likely to be closely attended by at least one male.

[ABOVE LEFT] Forms are nothing more than an area where the hare rests. The body of the animal presses and moulds the vegetation into a hare-shaped depression.

[ABOVE RIGHT] Young hares are precocial animals, only visited by their mother once every 24 hours, when they can suckle for about five minutes. They eat solid food from about two weeks of age.

A hare hopping across a field, with a second animal in close pursuit is the sign you are looking for here. Even when resting, the pair are likely to be near each other. While pairs are certainly worth keeping an eye on, larger concentrations of hares suggest that the female is close to being ready to mate, and that several males are all chancing their luck. This is the perfect setting for an amazing natural display, and ideal for observation.

If the location you are watching has a good network of small roads with safe stopping places, then watching from a car can be rewarding. Where there are public footpaths and other tracks where people regularly walk, the hares will be used to seeing (benign) people and so these too may prove ideal for observation. If hares spot you, even several hundred metres away, in a place where they do not normally see humans, they are very likely to run off in the opposite direction.

If you have identified a field or other area where the hares are regularly resting or feeding, this may be a good place to build a field hide (page 24) or put up a portable hide – with the landowner's permission, of course. If you do choose to use a hide, ensure that your field of view is as wide as possible. Once they get going, hares can be incredibly dynamic, covering many hundreds of metres in a very short time. You do not have to be especially careful about wind direction as hares, though using their sense of smell to identify the sexual state of a female, do not seem to respond to human scent.

A female nearing oestrus attended by several males is likely to settle
at some point in the early morning, and the males will then do the same,
in fairly close attendance. While it may look like the action is over for
the day, do not be fooled. If the female decides to move (and she almost
certainly will at some point) this will kick-start the action and once
again the whole troupe will follow her. These are the circumstances
that may lead to boxing bouts. Boxing – two hares facing each other
and rearing up to strike out with their forefeet at the opponent's face
and body – takes place between males and females, and is catalysed
by a male getting too close to a female who is not yet ready to mate. She
will turn on him, stand up on her hind legs and strike to force him away.

Most of the time he will take the hint and settle back a metre or so
away from her, but if there are several other males around, and/or if the
female is very close to being receptive, he may be more insistent with
his advances and rear up to face her, defending himself with his forefeet.
If he is really pushy, he will try to outmanoeuvre her, attempting to
approach her from behind, and she may wheel around in the air and
strike him with her powerful hind feet, often sending clumps of fur
flying. Males sometimes scuffle in the heat of the moment, but I have
never seen a protracted fight between two males.

Look out for lone hares that appear to be on a mission. Single males
that have picked up the scent of a female in season often abandon
feeding, and, with nose to the ground and ears forward, trot and hop

Sound	Sight	Smell
8	**10**	**3**

BROWN HARE'S YEAR

Mating: January–August

Gestation: 41–42 days

Young: 3 or 4 litters of 3 or
4 young (leverets) born from
February– October

[OPPOSITE] Hares have a remarkable
field of vision. Their bulging eyes are
set high and they can see movement
over almost a full 360° without having
to move their head.

through the fields trying to find the source of the alluring
perfume. These males seem to lose their usual timidity and
individuals have run within a couple of metres of where I
have been standing without flinching or looking up at me.
These males are likely to lead you to a receptive female or
a group of other males that have found a female in season.

If you manage to spot a hare in its form, then you may
be able to approach it by using a technique that looks as
though you are practising for the ministry of silly walks!
From a distance of more than 100 metres, first move around
so that you are broadside to the animal. Then, at a gentle
pace, walk towards it, ensuring that only one of its eyes can
see you. Try to minimise the usual up-and-down bobbing
action of walking, keeping your head and body in the same
vertical plane as you go. As you close the distance between
yourself and the hare, start bending your knees, a little at
first, then more so as you get closer. By progressively getting
shorter you give the impression to the hare that you are
staying still (remaining the same size), as without binocular
vision it finds it hard to judge your distance. There is a
critical distance at which sound and movement make it
obvious that you are creeping up on the unsuspecting
creature, and this varies from hare to hare, and according to
the stealth of your approach. Once a hare has left its form, it
may circle round and try to approach its favoured site once
again. Assuming you have moved to an acceptable distance
and hidden well, this habit may afford you some good views.

Female hares are often extremely nervous when they are
nursing young and must be treated with great care. The
young are left pretty much to their own devices for the
course of the day and only at dusk will the female come to a
regular spot where all the young gather for a very quick feed.
A female approaching this feeding place will not complete
her journey if she feels there is the slightest threat nearby.
If she feels the coast is clear, she makes the last few hops
to the site in a wildly erratic manner, often covering large
distances with each leap. This behaviour has almost
certainly evolved to break her scent, making it harder for
ground predators to follow. Suckling usually occurs when
it is very dark, and on occasion during the night (I have
only watched it in the very late evening during early June).

MOUNTAIN HARE *Lepus timidus*

SIGN

FOOTPRINTS

Prints are similar to those of the brown hare (page 148), with both fore and hind feet often appearing broader. The hind footprint has four toes, all forward facing and often with obvious claw marks. The length of the print varies a great deal, depending on the ground condition. On firm, damp soil it may only be 3cm long, looking a little like an odd cat print, especially if the claws don't register. On very wet soil or, as is more likely, in soft snow, it can be much longer, up to about 14 cm, as the whole rear heel leaves its mark.

The forefeet have five toes, but the inner toe rarely registers in a print. They measure about 4.5cm by 3cm, but may appear broader when running over snow as the hare splays its toes.

The gait pattern is the same as that of the brown hare, with forefeet running more or less in a straight line and hind feet leaving their impression just in front and on either side of the forefeet. The tracks of this species are more likely to be found than those of brown hare because of the hare's preference for living at altitude where snow is likely to fall.

SIZE
Weight: 2.5–3.5kg
Length to rump: 45–56cm
Tail length: 7cm

Front right print (actual size)

Rear right print (actual size)

Sound
8

Sight
10

Smell
3

MOUNTAIN HARE'S YEAR

Mating: February–August (peak March–July)

Gestation: 50 days

Young: 1–4 litters each year of 1–3 young born usually in March–July

[TOP] Due to the upland habitat of this species, tracks in snow are common.

[ABOVE] Droppings are scattered as the animal feeds. They are rounded, greenish and contain fibrous material.

Unlike deer and many other creatures, which usually walk across steep hills, mountain hares tend to run directly up and down steep slopes, and their tracks in snow betray this.

FAECES *Droppings*

These are virtually identical to brown hare faeces. When the hare is feeding mainly on heather shoots, its droppings contain dry, fibrous material and older droppings of this nature are a sandy brown. Otherwise, wetter foodstuffs produce darker, rather less fibrous droppings.

FOOD REMAINS

As for brown hare. The mountain hare prefers to eat grasses where available, but in the UK many feed mostly on heather and the shoots of willow and other low-growing upland plants.

HAIR

Mountain hares have a variable coat. In summer, the upper body, flanks and head are greyish-brown and the belly hair creamy white. As winter approaches, mountain hares moult into an all-white pelage which gives better camouflage (and possibly greater insulation) in snowy conditions.

HOME

Like their close relative the brown hare, mountain hares do not make a home as such, but when they rest, they settle into a patch of longer vegetation or a dip in the land or they scrape a shallow bed in the snow and lie within it. These forms are hard to discern in vegetation but in the snow they are quite obvious when fresh, especially since tracks lead to and from them. Snow forms may also have a channel, or short tunnel, dug in an arc away from the resting place. This may be used by the hare to avoid sudden attack by a predator.

HOW TO WATCH

Mountain hares can be watched using very similar methods of observation as brown hares. In some areas, mountain hares are less timid than their lowland cousins, and they may be much more confiding, allowing close observation. They may even trot up to the observer for a closer look.

HEDGEHOG *Erinaceus europaeus*

SIGN
FOOTPRINTS

Hedgehog prints are very rarely encountered in the field. When they do show, for example in wet mud, they almost always reveal only four of the five toes on both front and hind feet. Also, contrary to many illustrations (which seem to be based more on the shape of the foot than the way the prints appear in the wild), the extended heel of the hind foot rarely if ever shows, since it is raised as the animal walks. A walking or trotting hedgehog rises up on its toes as it moves and it is these toes, along with long narrow claws, that tend to leave an impression. Heel pads rarely leave anything more than the faintest of marks.

In normal walking gait, the toes of the right hind foot slightly overlap the heel pad of the right forefoot; the same applies to the left side track. Front and hind feet are roughly similar in size – just under 3cm wide and (bearing in mind the lack of a heel pad mark) 1.5–2cm long.

FAECES *Droppings*

While hedgehogs will eat the odd peanut (if offered) or other vegetable matter, they are insectivores. Beetles, earwigs,

SIZE
Male larger than female
Weight: up to 2kg (heaviest just prior to hibernation)
Length to rump: up to 30cm
Height at shoulder: 6–8cm

Front right print overstepped by rear right foot (actual size)

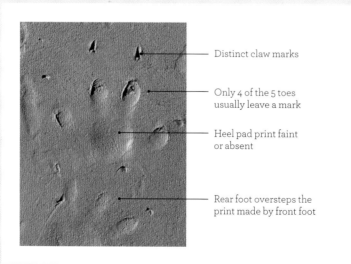

Distinct claw marks

Only 4 of the 5 toes usually leave a mark

Heel pad print faint or absent

Rear foot oversteps the print made by front foot

[OPPOSITE TOP] Hedgehogs are primarily nocturnal, though they do venture out to forage by day, especially early in the season or during dry periods when food is more scarce.

worms and other invertebrates make up the majority of their diet. Droppings are cylindrical, 2–3cm long by 1–1.5cm wide. They usually appear blackish, with lots of beetle chitin in the mix, much of it shining on the surface of the dropping. When hedgehogs have eaten lots of earthworms, slugs and snails, their droppings are looser and may contain soil (from the worms) or be more jelly-like from the molluscs.

FOOD REMAINS

Hedgehogs may raid the nests of ground-nesting birds at both the egg and chick stages. Eggs are usually eaten within the nest and you may find empty shells with clear holes or grooves cut into them by the jaws of the hedgehog and the contents lapped out by the raider's tongue. Carrion is taken, but feeding signs are ambiguous. Where snails are eaten (often late in the summer) shattered shells may be found at the feeding place.

Droppings are cylindrical and usually contain chewed beetle elytra and other invertebrate body parts.

HOME

Hedgehogs may spend the day in any quiet area with thick vegetation, under log piles, in gaps at the base of tree roots or similar retreats. They readily take to purpose-built hedgehog houses which offer dry sanctuary. With the onset of winter, they construct more substantial nests, often made with piles of dry leaves and grasses, in which to hibernate. These winter nests, or hibernacula, may be built in a few hours or over a number of days. There may be several used through the course of the winter, as the hedgehog may stir from its torpor on a number of occasions before becoming fully active the following spring.

Many hedgehogs are killed or injured every year as a result of gardening accidents. Piles of vegetation earmarked for a bonfire should be carefully turned over before setting them alight, since these provide the perfect nesting place for hedgehogs. Great care should be taken when strimming areas of deep, rough vegetation. A fearful hedgehog will not run from the sound of a strimmer, but instead curl into a defensive ball and, if not spotted, will suffer horrendous and often fatal injuries.

HOW TO WATCH

Hedgehogs are not usually very timid, though their reaction to human company does vary between individuals. In its normal passage through its territory, a hedgehog moves at a fairly brisk pace, rising up on its legs, with spines lying flat along its back. When foraging, its progress is slower and it tends to sit on its haunches more. If it feels threatened, it goes through various stages of drawing its spines over its face then body, and ultimately rolling into a tight ball, depending on the level of threat.

Hedgehogs are nocturnal creatures and, in suburban environments at least, they tend to be most active after midnight. You can, though, encounter a hedgehog at almost any time of day or night, especially at dawn when a foraging animal may still be out and about, having not found what it was looking for during the hours of darkness.

Generally, however, this is a night wanderer. Once you have established the presence of hedgehogs through their

HEDGEHOG SENSES

Sound	Sight	Smell
6	3	3

HEDGEHOG'S YEAR

Hibernation: October–late March

Mating: from early May–mid-August

Gestation: 31–35 days

Young: 1 litter of 4–6 young born in June; sometimes a second litter in September; young from summer litters wander outside nest from mid-June

sign, spend time in the territory after dark, using your ears more than your eyes. A relaxed hedgehog is a noisy eater, and one crunching through beetles, snails and other invertebrates will draw your attention. Even while searching for a meal, the snuffles and snorts a hedgehog makes in the undergrowth can be remarkably loud for such a diminutive creature and can lead you to it. If you are using a torch, cover the lens with red gel to reduce disturbance.

Hedgehog hearing is reasonably acute so take care as you walk or move close to an animal. Be aware of your outline and try not stand out too starkly against the sky from the hogs' perspective. Despite their noisy habits, they can be very hard to spot, especially in thick vegetation, so patience and a good eye are required for protracted views. Keep a distance of 3–5 metres between you and the hog, and if you find that the one you are following keeps its spines partially erect, or continually stops and adopts a defensive position, either increase your following distance, or give up and find another subject.

Hedgehogs readily come to food and water proffered in shallow bowls. You can buy proprietary hedgehog food, but hogs are also partial to wet dog and cat food (beef or chicken based rather than fish). Do not feed them bread and milk – it gives them diarrhoea and makes them very sick.

MOLE *Talpa europaea*

You are most unlikely to encounter a mole above ground, and if you do, it will be thanks to serendipity rather than any fieldcraft technique. Nor will you find droppings or feeding sign other than the familiar molehills.

SIGN

Moles dig extensive underground tunnel systems where they spend almost their entire lives. Environmental drivers that cause moles to come to the surface include drought and flood; behavioural events leading to brief surface eruptions are chases between individuals, the collection of nest material and over-enthusiastic foraging close to the surface.

For the most part, moles betray their presence through their excavation activities – their hills, tunnels and furrows. Large molehills are usually centres of activity beneath which there may be a nest. Smaller hills are the result of foraging activities.

SIZE
Male larger than female
Weight: 100g
Length to rump: 14.5cm
Tail length: 3.3cm

MOLE SENSES

Sound
8

Sight
1

Smell
9

[ABOVE LEFT] Surface burrows are common but usually well hidden under grasses and other vegetation. This burrow crosses an area of open ground, revealing its twisting pathway.

[ABOVE RIGHT] While moles are invisible for the most part, their earthworks are anything but. Molehills are a familiar sight over much of the UK.

HOW TO WATCH

In areas of high mole activity you can watch them working, even if you never lay eyes on the animals themselves.

Choose an area of short vegetation where the spoil heaps are numerous and at least some are very fresh. Stand (or better still, sit) in the centre of the most active area and watch the hills and earth around you. This is best done at dawn. Be certain to keep completely still. Any movement of your feet or body sends vibrations through the soil which warn the mole that there is something above ground that could be a danger; they will cease all digging activity until they feel secure – which may be several hours. With patience, you will see earth moving and being pushed to the surface of hills and may see surface tunnels being raised as the mole forages through the root tangle. With good fortune, you may catch a glimpse of a mole as it breaks the surface, either through the centre of a hill or as it forages very close to the surface.

Moles are taken by many predators and they feature as regular prey items of several species, especially common buzzards and barn owls. Mammalian predators may kill a mole if they come across it, but they frequently leave their kill without eating it. This suggests that they find the insectivore distasteful in much the same way as the mole's cousins, the shrews, tend to be abandoned.

SHREWS

Shrews are highly strung little insectivores that live life in the fast lane. The two most common species in the UK are the common shrew and the pygmy shrew. Both are terrestrial and live a life hidden from view for the most part on the woodland floor and rough grassland.

The water shrew favours freshwater habitats, but is equally at home in the ground cover of woodland and rough grassland.

In Britain, the lesser white-toothed shrew occurs on the Isles of Scilly and the Channel Islands, where it tends to forage on the seashore, particularly in dunes or on the strandline, searching for amphipods, flies and their larvae.

SIGN
FOOTPRINTS

If you are lucky enough to come across a shrew footprint – and they are such light animals and almost always move through vegetation so the chances are minuscule – it can be told apart from a mouse or vole print because it has five toes on the front foot, not four. Otherwise shrew footprints are virtually indistinguishable from the prints of the little rodents.

The water shrew lives in freshwater habitats and their margins and so it is this species that is most likely to leave a print in the soft mud alongside a pond or brook. Each footprint is made with the whole of the foot (plantigrade) and has five splayed toes, each bearing claw marks. The hind foot can leave quite an elongate mark, with rear heel pads sitting well back from the toes. All this is relative of course! Pygmy shrew prints are about 5mm long from heel to toe and even the largest species, the water shrew, leaves prints no longer than 10mm.

WATER SHREW
Neomys fodiens
Weight: 12–18g; length to rump: 67–95mm;
tail length: 45–77mm

COMMON SHREW
Sorex araneus
Weight: 5–14g; length to rump: 48–80mm;
tail length: 24–44mm

PYGMY SHREW
Sorex minutus
Weight: 2.5–6g; length to rump: 40–60mm;
tail length: 323–45mm

Droppings are minute, especially those of the pygmy shrew. This water shrew dropping contains fragments of beetles and other invertebrates.

FAECES *Droppings*

Droppings are tiny – about 2mm long for a pygmy shrew, 4mm long for a water shrew – and 1–2mm thick. They are tapered at both ends and tend to be blackish, usually containing insect remains. You can find them by turning logs or refugia.

FOOD REMAINS

All shrews are voracious hunters of invertebrates, taking everything from earthworms to earwigs and beetles. Water shrews feed on any terrestrial invertebrates, but they are also powerful swimmers and divers, so can catch aquatic bugs as well as the odd fish and amphibian. Prey remains are scarce, almost all kills being eaten in their entirety. Water shrews sometimes leave the guts and fins of small fish on a rock or bank where they have fed. They also take water snails from time to time and crushed shells may be piled on the bank or near the entrance of a burrow.

HOME

Water shrews dig burrow systems into the banks of brooks or standing water. The entrance to the burrow is small – about 2cm across – and is wider than it is high. When a shrew enters, it has to squeeze into the burrow and this action may help the animal rid itself of excessive moisture. Otherwise this species, and other shrews, use existing burrow systems, runs through vegetation and cover such as logs and rock piles to build nests and generally move around their feeding grounds.

Pygmy shrews rarely wander further than a 30 metre radius. Water shrews travel much more widely, settling for a few days or weeks in one patch before moving on as a loose colony or family group.

HOW TO WATCH

Shrews are hard to see in the wild. They stick to deep cover for the most part and at best you catch only a glimpse of them as they dash across a path or other open space. Young ears can hear shrew calls, which are uttered as the shrew moves through vegetation and may be a rudimentary form of echolocation. Calls tend to be in the 4–8kHz range (at the upper limit of human hearing) and most people are able to hear them up to the age of 35–40. Women tend to maintain their higher-frequency hearing capacity until later in life than men. I lost the ability to hear shrews when I reached 40. Calls are a piercing, sibilant twittering, often starting with a longer note, then followed by rapidly uttered chirps. Shrew calls register well on a bat detector set at low frequency.

Your most likely sighting of a shrew is finding one lying dead in the middle of a path or on a rock or log. This is a surprisingly common occurrence and takes place because shrews produce a foul-tasting substance from glands on their flanks. Naive predators, like young foxes, sometimes catch shrews thinking they have found a mouse, and kill it before they realise they have made a mistake. They don't eat it but let it drop, sometimes in the open. Some owls, especially barn owls, are not affected by the shrew's defence and so can feed on them with impunity.

Water shrews are just as hard to see in terrestrial habitats as their cousins, but when they are feeding near to or in water you have much more opportunity to observe them. If you are young enough to hear the shrews' calls, you will discover that they are very vocal as they move around the bankside vegetation and also highly visible as they forage along the bank or dive in search of food.

If you spot a water shrew, the chances are it will be accompanied by others; they frequently move in small family parties. Watch from a distance at first to familiarise yourself with the areas of water they are focusing on, then move in for a closer look. As long as you do not cast your shadow across them, and take care not to move suddenly when they are near, you can get very close protracted views. In clear water, you can see water shrews foraging underwater, appearing silvery as a result of the layer of trapped air in their fine coat. I have used a mask and snorkel to get really close views in the past, and had shrews come to investigate my submerged hands.

SHREW SENSES

Sound	Sight	Smell
5	2	2

SHREW'S YEAR

Shrews do not hibernate. Lifespan for all three species discussed here is 1–1.5 years.

Most shrews that overwinter are immature, maturing rapidly the following spring.

Breeding occurs through the summer months with 2–4 litters of 5 or 6 young on average.

The water shrew [OPPOSITE TOP] is the largest of the species in the UK, with the pygmy shrew [BOTTOM LEFT] the smallest, as the name suggests, and the common shrew [BOTTOM RIGHT] midway between them.

BATS

Of the 18 species of bat in the UK (17 of which are known to breed here) many are wholly nocturnal, only emerging from their day roosts under the cover of complete darkness. For most species, observation in the field is challenging, though there are a few that venture forth at dusk and dawn. All can be monitored with a bat detector.

I am going to detail only the species that you are likely to be able to observe at dusk or dawn, with brief reference to the monitoring of other species using a bat detector.

All bat species are protected by law in the UK and it is an offence to disturb them or to damage or destroy a bat roosting place, even if they are not using it at the time.

SIGN
FAECES *Droppings*
Bats betray their presence by the droppings beneath their roosts. These are black or dark brown, often slightly shiny, and look very like the droppings of a mouse – tapered at both ends and bullet shaped. Size varies according to species. The smallest are about 4mm long, produced by the pipistrelle; the largest, from noctule and greater horseshoe bats, are 7–10mm long. Unlike mouse droppings, these are dry and readily crumble to a fine dust under slight pressure. With gloved hands, you can conduct the crumble test between finger and thumb.

Close inspection will reveal the presence of insect remains, such as the elytra (hard wing covers) of beetles or fragments of legs and wings of other insect species, though these are chewed to a fine powder. A small quantity of droppings has little scent, but large roosts, especially nursery roosts where many females gather to give birth and raise young, may become so soiled that a distinctive aroma, heavy with ammonia, may develop.

Some bats, such as the long-eared and the horseshoe bats, bring larger prey items back to a favourite night roosting site where they devour the soft body parts, dropping the more indigestible bits to the floor below. A litter of

Droppings, or guano, vary in size from species to species. These lesser horseshoe bat droppings are about 5mm long by 2mm wide. They contain the hard remains of invertebrate prey.

A lesser horseshoe bat. Several bat species have favourite resting places that they use from time to time throughout the night while they digest and groom. These are distinct from their sleeping quarters.

cockchafer heads and elytra may be a sign that a greater horseshoe bat has been feeding, whereas the wings of some moth species, particularly yellow underwing, may suggest the feeding roost of a long-eared bat.

DETECTION AND OBSERVATION

Large roosts can be quite noisy, especially at dusk and dawn when the colony communicates using sounds that fall within the range of human hearing. The mechanical sounds produced by the bats' fidgeting within a roost may also be audible from a significant distance. Ultrasonic calls, which are used by bats to 'see' the world about them using echolocation, are too high-pitched for human hearing.

However, these calls can be a great aid to finding and identifying bats with a bat detector. The most commonly used of these devices is the heterodyne type, which uses an ultrasonic microphone to pick up the bat calls and mixes them with the output of a high-frequency oscillator. This produces a sound on an inbuilt speaker that is the sum (and difference) of the two frequencies. Each bat species calls within a certain frequency range, and so with practice it is possible to identify which you are listening to. The rhythm and pattern of each species call varies too and there are good resources online to check the calls made by each as heard on a heterodyne bat detector.

BAT'S YEAR

All bat species in the UK hibernate in winter, often in caves, sometimes in the cellars of buildings or in hollow trees. Most are dormant from the first frosts in October to the last frosts in late March or April, though any bat may emerge through the winter if conditions become warm enough.

Females form nursery roosts in the early spring (the location of these varies according to the species), gathering in noisy colonies to give birth. Males tend to stay solitary or in small groups.

Young are born in midsummer, usually June. They stay clinging to their mother and feeding on her milk for several weeks before they are fully furred and able to move around the colony independently.

In early autumn (September), the young bats start to hunt for themselves and the adults' thoughts once more turn to breeding. Mating takes place over the next month or two, with males attracting mates by special calls. This period is also crucial for all bats to build up fat reserves so that they can survive the rigours of hibernation.

By November, most bats are hibernating.

PIPISTRELLE
Pipistrellus pipistrellus

SIZE
Weight: 3–8g
Length: 3.5–4.5cm
Wingspan: 20–23.5cm

There are three species of pipistrelle in the UK but this one, together with the very similar soprano pipistrelle (*Pipistrellus pygmaeus*), is the most common by far. They are small bats, with a rapid, jerky flight, and together they represent the most common bat species in the region.

Pipistrelles often roost in the roofs of buildings, especially behind soffit boards, and can squeeze into remarkably narrow gaps in very large numbers. Prior to emergence they often become excited and vocal, using calls that can be heard by the human ear. Large roosts may produce a strong scent that may pervade the living space of a house. The area beneath these roosts becomes peppered with droppings.

This species often starts flying before it has become completely dark, and it is possible to conduct counts by watching the emergence at dusk. Hunting flights are often at about roof height or lower, with the bat dipping and twisting each time it chases a flying insect. One pipistrelle may consume more than 3,000 small insects in a single night!

NOCTULE
Nyctalus noctula

SIZE
Weight: 18–40g
Length: 3.7–4.8cm
Wingspan: 32–40cm

One of the largest bats in the region, noctules are powerful flyers, often leaving their roost while the sky is still very light, sometimes even before sunset. They fly high and with a purposeful, direct line, dipping suddenly to snatch an insect, then resuming their high hunting flight.

This species can be heard by children (and some lucky adults) without the aid of a detector, since its calls may fall as low as 20 kHz, peaking at 25 kHz. I lost my ability to hear them without the help of a bat detector in my early thirties – a sad day! When I was still able to hear them unaided, the call was a ringing, metallic squeak, almost insect-like, and though I could tell it was coming from the sky it was often hard to pinpoint the exact direction

It was while watching noctules hunting high over a lake at dusk that I was privy to their predator evasion tactics. Noctules and other bat species are sometimes targeted by hobbies – mercurial birds of prey that specialise in taking aerial prey items, like dragonflies, swallows and martins. The bats were hawking high

over the water when I heard them emit a shrill, very rapid call. Collectively they suddenly dipped down towards the water, and spread out in a starburst. Immediately behind them was a narrow-winged bird which, it turned out, was a black-headed gull and not a hobby. I assumed, however, that from the bats' point of view it was a case of 'better safe than sorry' and that they had communicated a suspected danger and had taken evasive action accordingly.

Noctules tend to roost in trees, often in old woodpecker holes or rot holes. Such roosts rarely show physical signs of occupation, but this species can be noisy, chattering at dusk in frequencies audible to most people and so drawing attention to their roost. Flights from roost sites to hunting areas are high, fast and direct.

DAUBENTON'S BAT
Myotis daubentonii

SIZE
Weight: 7–12g
Length: 4.5– 5.5cm
Wingspan: 24– 27.5cm

Sometimes referred to as the water bat, this medium-sized species has a close affinity with wetland habitats. If you see a bat fluttering low and close to the surface of a river, pond or canal, it is very likely to be Daubenton's, which can appear to almost touch the water surface from time to time. In fact, these bats have been known to snatch insects from the water with their feet, sometimes using their tail membrane as a scoop.

The Daubenton's summer roosts are often in cavities and crannies under bridges or other holes close to water and any droppings produced may fall directly into the water, making detection tricky. Vocalisation is high frequency and low intensity, making unaided detection challenging.

GREATER HORSESHOE BAT
Rhinolophus ferrumequinum

SIZE
Weight: 17–34g
Length: 5.7– 7.1cm
Wingspan: 35–40cm

This is a chunky bat whose summer nursery roosts are sometimes in caves but often in the large roof spaces of older buildings or in underground tunnels. Such roosts are noisy affairs, with lots of chattering and squeaking calls that fall well within the range of human hearing.

The bats emerge within half an hour of sunset and so are quite visible against a summer sky at dusk. They conduct much of their feeding by hanging upside down on a favoured perch – typically the branch of a tree – and scanning for suitable prey before dashing out to capture it. Larger prey, such as cockchafer beetles, are brought back to the perch to be eaten, and litters of beetle wings and other insect parts may be found beneath a well-used site. Droppings may be found beneath these hunting perches and large piles of droppings collect beneath day roosts.

This species is particularly sensitive to disturbance and any suspected roost must be left well alone. Observation of roost exodus points should be conducted quietly and at a reasonable distance.

LESSER HORSESHOE BAT
Rhinolophus hipposideros

SIZE
Weight: 5–9g
Length: 3.5–4.5cm
Wingspan: 20–25cm

Like its larger cousin, the lesser horseshoe hangs from its roost point in closely knit summer colonies. This may be in roof spaces, caves or other secluded spaces with even to warm temperatures. Though vocal, these bats have softer, higher voices than the greater horseshoe bat which makes them less likely to draw attention to themselves.

These bats emerge within half an hour of sunset and fly low, fluttering over vegetation and sometimes gleaning their insect prey from leaves and grasses. Many seek a temporary night roost where they return to rest, digest and sometimes feed on larger prey. These night roosts may be in trees but are often in the open porches of buildings.

Litters of droppings mixed with occasional insect remains on the floor of a porch are a sign that this species is in residence through the hours of darkness.

SEROTINE
Eptesicus serotinus

SIZE
Weight: 15–35g
Length: 5.8–8cm
Wingspan: 32–38cm

The serotine often emerges at dusk when there is lots of light still in the sky, returning to its roost when dawn has well and truly broken. Summer roosts are often in roof spaces, or in gaps between tiles or crevices in walls. Prior to emergence, serotines fidget and chatter, and both their mechanical and vocal sounds can catch your attention.

Immediately after emergence, the bats frequently flutter back and forth near the roost exit, and the reverse is true as they return at dawn, flying to and fro before finally settling and entering their roost site.

In flight the serotine has a relaxed, leisurely appearance, its broad wings rowing through the air – often quite low down around tree branches and grassland. Well-used roosts may have slight discolouration where the bats' bodies repeatedly rub past the entrance, and droppings may gather beneath sites that are vertically situated.

WHALES AND DOLPHINS

WHITE-SIDED DOLPHIN
Weight: up to 165kg; length: up to 2.5m

BOTTLENOSE DOLPHIN
Weight: up to 275kg; length: up to 2.7m

ORCA
Weight: up to 5,000kg; length: up to 9.5m

COMMON DOLPHIN
Weight: up to 85kg; length: up to 2.4m

RISSO'S DOLPHIN
Weight: up to 400kg; length: up to 3.8m

Whale and dolphin encounters are, with a few notable exceptions, matters of chance. Certainly, there are seasons and stretches of coastline where the likelihood of a view is increased, but there are few field skills which improve your chances, besides knowledge of the coastline, good observational skills and plenty of patience.

Weather conditions make a tremendous difference to your chances of spotting one of these animals. Try to pick a day with little or no wind, since choppy water can camouflage the low profile of even a large whale surfacing to breathe. Lighting conditions are important too. Strangely perhaps, bright overhead sunlight is not ideal, since it does nothing to reveal the form of a surfacing animal. Better is flat but bright cloud cover or perhaps a backlight that helps show a surfacing animal as a silhouette against an otherwise bright waterscape.

Unless you are visiting a known place of high activity, get on to some high ground so you can scan as big an expanse of water as possible.

Look out for gatherings of seabirds. They may be attracted to cetacean feeding activity, which forces fish close to the surface and within reach of birds like gannets and gulls.

Species you can expect to see close inshore include bottlenose and Risso's dolphins, porpoise and orca. Other species, such as white-sided and common dolphins, are more likely to be encountered further out to sea, though such is the dynamic nature of this group of animals and the environment they inhabit, that there is a chance of seeing any species in almost any part of the ocean.

ORCA
Orcinus orca

Orcas are an increasingly frequent sight along northern coasts. Hot spots for inshore sightings in the British Isles are Shetland and Orkney, though encounters around Hebridean islands and along other parts of the Scottish coastline are becoming more common, as are occasional records further south.

Inshore sightings are most likely to occur from May through to August when common (harbour) seals congregate to have their pups. Mid-June sees the highest concentration of newborn seal pups in the northern isles, and the orca make the most of this seasonal glut. In late summer orcas commonly move offshore to target the mackerel fishing fleets in the North Sea. At the time of writing, orcas do not appear specifically to prey on grey seals during their breeding season in the autumn.

HOW TO WATCH

As with all whales and dolphins, orcas are unpredictable. A chance encounter may take place at any time of year. Watch for the blow over the sea (vapour hanging on the air from the forceful exhalation of a surfacing animal) or for their dorsal fins. Adult male orcas have dorsal fins that may measure 1.8 metres and so can be very eye-catching. Juveniles and females have smaller dorsal fins but they all show up well when surfacing to breathe.

During the summer months, orcas visit traditional common seal pupping sites, but just which day they will choose to turn up is impossible to predict.

If you are lucky enough to encounter an orca or a pod working close to shore, it is sometimes possible to track them by leapfrogging to the next bay or headland in their direction of travel. Do not underestimate their speed! If they disappear around a headland, there is a very good chance they will be a bay or two further on than you expect before your next encounter.

If you are on foot, it is impossible to keep up with a fast-moving pod. Using a vehicle to loop ahead in their direction of travel can prove very effective. Be patient when adopting this method. Orcas that are successful when targeting seals may take their kill further offshore to eat it, then move back inshore to look for another meal.

A range of hunting techniques is used by these cooperative and seemingly intelligent animals. In British waters I have observed orcas creating waves to wash young pups and even adult seals from rocks into the sea where they can grab them. Many kills are made beneath the surface. Watch for the orcas apparently hanging in the water, arching their bodies with heads pointing down – a sure sign that they are either searching for a seal hiding in the seaweed or have already made a kill and are feeding.

If you see orcas while you are in a boat, give them the respect they are due and do not pursue them. It may be possible to arc ahead in their direction of travel by a kilometre or so, then allow the boat to lie in slack water as they cruise by you. Observation from a sea kayak can be exhilarating and extremely close!

BOTTLENOSE DOLPHIN
Tursiops truncatus

Second only to the harbour porpoise in frequency of sightings are bottlenose dolphins, which can be seen off almost any stretch of coastline around the British Isles and beyond. Well-known pods display remarkable site fidelity, and there are some locations around the British coast that have established reputations for hosting a local family or pod which can be seen week on week, year on year. Bottlenose dolphin boat tours, especially in Scotland and Wales, often enjoy the spectacle of bow-riding animals and in some places shore-based viewings may be extremely regular at surprisingly close quarters.

As with other cetaceans, look out for this dolphin's dorsal fins breaking the surface, or even full body breaches – a trait common in this species. In favoured hunting grounds, such as those along the Scottish east coast, you may have shore-based views as the dolphins target migratory salmon and sea trout, which tend to follow the coastline on their way to their freshwater breeding grounds.

As with all cetaceans, a strict code of conduct should be followed if watching bottlenose dolphins from a boat so as not to disturb them. Guidelines can be found on the Sea Watch Foundation website.

Sub-aquatic encounters with bottlenose dolphins (or any other cetaceans) in British, Irish or European waters should be avoided, partly due to poor visibility and also because of the species' reluctance to spend protracted periods close to a swimming human in these regions. There have been notable exceptions to this trait, but being repeatedly pursued by humans in boats or dropping humans into the water close to the pods, may affect the behaviour of dolphins and other cetaceans and be detrimental to the animals' wellbeing.

[OPPOSITE] While the most common views of bottlenose dolphins are brief glimpses of the dorsal fin and blow hole as they surface to breathe, they occasionally put on spectacular displays – perhaps just because they can!

SEALS

Both our resident seal species come on to land throughout the year to rest and moult, as well as during their breeding seasons.

In open water, both may be confiding and curious towards a swimming human. Just how confiding varies hugely and depends on the population's experiences of human interaction.

There is little opportunity for the identification of sign. Wherever there are marks left in coastal sand by a seal, the chances are that you will see the animal nearby. Such tracks show the front limbs as five toed with very broad palms held to the side of the body, which leaves a pronounced drag mark.

Almost all droppings and food remains are deposited in the sea, apart from in grey seal breeding colonies, which can become heavily soiled with a build-up of faecal matter.

Both species are visible when breeding, though the grey seal spends a great deal more time on land than does its smaller cousin.

SEAL HAUL-OUTS

Seals haul out on traditionally used rocks, man-made structures or beaches. Many of these are covered by water at high tide and seals may linger on a haul-out until the tide washes them off. During moulting periods, the process of hauling out allows the blood vessels close to the surface of the skin to flood and heat up, aiding the process of moulting and generally allowing the seal to rest and relax by conserving body heat. When the seal is swimming in cold water, these blood vessels close down, maintaining core temperature behind the layer of blubber. It is likely that the growth of new hair is inhibited at this time.

Grey and common seals will haul out on coastal rocks and quiet shores at any time of year when conditions are reasonably clement. Where both

GREY SEAL
Halichoerus grypus
Weight: M up to 310kg; F up to 186kg
Length: M 2.45m; F 2.2m

COMMON SEAL
Phoca vitulina
Weight: M up to 130kg; F up to 106kg
Length: M 1.85m; F 1.75m

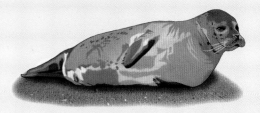

[OPPOSITE] Grey seals frequently haul out on a dropping tide. As the tide rises, they do their best to keep their tail flippers and heads clear of the chilling water.

species occur, they frequently share hauling-out spots, though there is likely to be some species-specific zoning in the grouping. Most hauling out begins on the falling tide and ends on the rising tide. In areas of broad sandbars, such as in the Wash in England, large numbers of common seals may haul out together on the briefly exposed land, following the tide line down as the tide shrinks back. This ensures they have rapid access to the water should they feel threatened.

Some traditional hauling-out sites are very close to the shoreline (for example, on Islay, Shetland and other islands) and the seals here have become used to the close company of humans. In more remote hauling-out points, however, seals can be very nervous and dash into the water at the merest hint of a human approaching. Repeated disturbance of this nature can adversely affect the wellbeing of the animals and should be avoided.

Common seals haul out communally, usually from two hours before low tide to two hours afterwards. Hauling out plays a role in thermoregulation, moulting, mating, giving birth and nursing young. It is also a way of avoiding predators – such as orcas in UK waters.

Grey seal pups are born on remote beaches in autumn. Their white fur may be a legacy of post-glacial Britain, camouflaging them on sea ice.

GREY SEAL

In Britain, this species breeds in the autumn, with cows coming ashore to traditional pupping grounds in September or October. Pups are born on land, and remain there, their mother tending them and allowing them to suckle until they take their first swim at three or four weeks old.

Soon after giving birth, the cow comes into season and bulls jostle and fight for the right to mate. Implantation of the blastocyst is delayed and gestation starts the following spring, taking about 215 days.

There are a number of well-known grey seal rookeries around the British coastline, many of which can be visited for superb views of the occupants. Always keep to footpaths and stick to site guidelines to ensure females are not accidentally separated from their newborn young. In more remote rookeries, extreme caution should be taken to make sure the animals are not disturbed. A slow, quiet approach is essential and keep your profile low and hidden at all times.

COMMON SEAL

This species usually gives birth in June or July on a rock or sandbar that will be covered by high water. As a result, pups swim within 12 hours of being born, and often sooner. Very young pups are supported by their mother on her back or with her front flippers once they enter the water, and suckling takes place on haul outs or in shallows for 40–60 minutes a day at low water.

Mating takes places soon after pups are born, followed by a period of delayed implantation of two to three months, and pups are born ten or eleven months after mating.

Common seals are generally nervous in their traditional pupping grounds and great care must be taken not to put undue stress on new mothers already tested by giving birth. Observation from the shore or a boat should be conducted at a good distance and at the first sign of an animal in the group becoming nervous, the observer should move away.

Grey seals (in the background above) and common seals (foreground) sometimes share hauling-out rocks. When they are side by side it is easy to compare their physical differences.

Sound
6

Sight
8

Smell
5

COMMON SEAL'S YEAR

Mating: June/July

Gestation: 10–11 months, including a 2–3 month delayed implantation

Young: single pup born in mid-June on intertidal rocks, or even in water; able to swim and dive from birth

GREY SEAL'S YEAR

Mating: October/November

Gestation: delayed implantation of 125 days, followed by 215 day gestation

Young: single pup born above tideline in October/November; suckled for about 20 days before being abandoned by mother; pups then make their way to the water to fend for themselves

HOW TO WATCH

SINGING TO SEALS

Both grey and common seals are curious by nature and will check out an unknown form on the shore. If that form also happens to be making a strange sound, their curiosity often gets the better of them and they will come very close indeed to listen and look. I have sung, played the whistle, attempted to play the violin (very poorly) and done a strange jig when being observed by seals spy-hopping in the water, and all these actions have brought at least some of my audience closer to shore to check me out. Often, when an individual gets very near, it will turn and submerge with a sudden splash, only to resurface a little way off and swim back on the surface towards me.

Though this behaviour is no more nor less than a display of the seals' natural curiosity, it does look for all the world as though they are genuinely interested in what I am doing. Probably no one else is!

SEALS IN THE WATER

I have filmed and watched both British species in their true marine element. Some individuals are highly strung and nervous; others can be confiding, even cheeky, in their behaviour. I have had both common and grey seals come very close indeed underwater, even nipping at my fins and putting their faces near to mine to look into my eyes through my diving mask. No special techniques are required for observation, other than having respect for the seals' independence and allowing them to call the shots rather than trying to pursue them.

I have found that singing into a snorkel or a diving demand valve can pique the curiosity of a seal, coaxing it closer for a good look at the strangely clumsy visitor to their sub-aquatic world.

BARN OWL *Tyto alba*

SIGN

NEST

Barn owls are currently protected under schedule 1 of the Wildlife and Countryside Act 1981 and it is an offence to disturb the species at or near a nest site without a licence.

Barn owls nest in cavities and covered areas. As their name suggests, in the UK and Europe they have a strong affinity with outbuildings, in particular older barns, as nesting and roosting places. They use abandoned first-floor platforms or the ledges where rafters meet thick stone walls to raise a family. Modern steel-framed barns offer fewer nesting opportunities but nest boxes are readily occupied and can make a huge difference to the population and breeding success of barn owls in an area where older, more traditional buildings have been lost. Besides ledges in buildings and purpose-built boxes, barn owls nest in the gaps between stacks of hay or straw bales, in hollow trees and in fissures in large rock faces.

No nest structure is built, but single birds or pairs may roost in a potential nest site over the winter. As the egg-laying period approaches, the owls start to break many of the cast pellets (see below) that have accumulated in the nest site. Using their beaks, they fragment the bone and fur bundles to create a fine mat over the entire floor.

During incubation it may be very difficult to establish the presence of a breeding pair unless they are flushed. But flushing a brooding owl by day can very easily lead to the eggs becoming abandoned and chilled, especially early on in the incubation period, so should be avoided at all costs.

OTHER SIGN

Like all owls (and many other bird species), barn owls cast pellets of undigested material from the kills they have made. A typical pellet is quite smooth and glossy looking when fresh, duller and more matt when older, and often very dark or almost black in colour. The form is cylindrical and rather rounded at both ends, measuring 3–6cm long by about 3cm across. Bone fragments do not usually show up a great deal

SIZE
Weight: 300g
Length: 34cm
Wingspan: 86cm

Barn owl pellets are rounded and dark, and fresh pellets have a glossy sheen. Contents usually include small mammal skulls and other bones, knitted together with the hair of prey.

on the surface of the pellet. Pellets are found beneath traditional roosting places in buildings or in cavities, and a considerable number may collect beneath frequently used roosting sites. Barn owls usually cast one or two pellets every 24 hours, and a count of pellets at a roost site gives some indication of how often the perch has been used.

Dissected pellets may contain the remains of large numbers of field and bank voles, shrews and wood mice. Small mammal skulls are likely to be intact, with little or no damage to the cranium (since small prey is swallowed whole). Birds feature much less frequently in the diet of barn owls than in some other owl species, but locally common species (such as starlings taken from a winter roost) may predominate in the pellets of some owls. If the owl has been eating birds, then entire feathers will be in the pellet, which is likely to be rounded at one end and tapering off with longer feathers at the other, creating a dart-like effect. Droppings may collect beneath roosting places, though since these are ejected in a projectile fashion, they are rarely found on top of the pellets, which tend to drop directly beneath the roosting point. Droppings are off-white to yellow-white, and due to their emission, frequently streak walls or floors near roost sites with 'squirt' traces.

Feathers from barn owls may be found at roosting and nesting sites as birds moult late in the summer.

HOW TO WATCH

Like most owl species, barn owls are predominantly nocturnal so most of their activity cycle goes unseen. However, when food is hard to come by or there is pressure to find more prey while raising chicks, barn owls readily hunt in broad daylight. This is especially true in the British Isles, both in summer when the days are long and in winter, when vole populations are reduced and climatic conditions (colder weather) mean the birds need a higher calorific intake. In equatorial regions seeing a barn owl hunting in daylight is virtually unheard of. By the way, barn owls are one of the most widely distributed of all birds.

In the UK, barn owls adopt a variety of strategies for hunting their small mammal prey. While there is still light in the sky, they regularly quarter long grass meadows and verges at low level, relying on their extremely low wing loading to maintain a slow ground speed in order to check the area thoroughly. While they do respond to visual cues, they rely predominantly on their exceptional sense of hearing to pinpoint their prey, either responding to the mechanical sounds made by small creatures moving in the grass or, more often, to minute squeaks and

Barn owls usually fly into a headwind while hunting, keeping their ground speed to a minimum. For the best head-on views, make sure the wind comes from behind you – owls are not affected by human scent.

other vocalisations produced by their prey. A barn owl reacts rapidly to such sounds, and, once it has located its prey, plummets into the grass head first, only pulling its head back and thrusting its talons forward at the very last moment before impact.

If you spot a barn owl hunting over open country it is very likely that the bird will visit the same site repeatedly, giving you the perfect opportunity for observation.

Stake-out observation techniques are very effective. Dress in drab or camouflage clothing and consider your outline when waiting, using existing vegetation or man-made structures to break up your shape. For evening watches, arrive on site at least an hour or more before sunset. Consider the wind direction carefully, not from the point of view of scent (barn owls do not respond negatively to the smell of a human), but rather to get the best view of the bird. Check that the wind is blowing from you towards the owl, since the bird will invariably head into the wind while quartering to ensure the slowest possible progress over the ground. At the end of each sweep, the owl will allow the wind to carry it back swiftly to the next starting position before coming slowly into the wind again.

Don't be tempted to move about while the bird is hunting. Be patient, watching the terrain and vegetation to maximise your chances of a close encounter, and you will almost certainly be rewarded.

For an even more intimate encounter you could consider being a vole. Almost literally! Barn owls can be duped into thinking they have heard a vole squeak and come very close indeed to an observer for a look. I have used this method from the open window of a parked vehicle, while standing near a hedgerow and even when lying flat in the middle of a long grass meadow. The latter technique can result in a vole's eye view of the bird as it hovers just a couple of metres over your face, scrutinising you before realising its error and flying on.

Once you have found a meadow that is regularly visited by a hunting owl, move into the centre of the long grass either at first light or well ahead of sunset. Sit down in the grass and keep watch. If the habitat is good, only your head and shoulders should show above the seed heads of the grasses. When you see that the owl is moving into the area to hunt, lie flat on your back, face to the sky. Staying as motionless as possible, mimic a vole squeak by making a short, sharp kissing sound. It helps to listen to a recording of field voles (there are examples online) and trying to perfect your 'squeak' before attempting to use it in the field. It is important to produce a sufficiently loud squeak, often enough for the owl to hear you, but not so often that it sounds artificial. Try leaving gaps of at least 10–15 seconds between short bursts of squeaking.

Barn owl flight is silent – they, like many other owls, have fine fringes along the leading edge of their primary feathers which buffer the sound made as they flap. The first sign you will have that your mimicry has been successful is the moment the owl comes into view – and this can be very close indeed! I have never had a bird actually land on my face while doing this, but on one or two occasions it has come very near. I have also had barn owls land on the roof rack of a car in which I was squeaking and study the ground next to the driver's door for signs of the mini-mammal that made the sound. Once you have seen the owl, stop the duplicity and allow it to go back to the serious business of hunting. In fact, once the owl has realised that the strange squeaking sound was being made by a human, it is unlikely ever to be fooled again.

Early in the nesting season, while male owls are establishing territory, they patrol on the wing, calling from time to time. It is possible to mimic these loud shrieking calls and bring an owl close to your hiding place. Listen carefully to recordings of the call then, using a sudden expulsion of air through your teeth, half hiss, half whistle to perfect your mimicry. Barn owl tend to call around their territory only after dark, but if you hear one, call back and watch for the silhouette of the bird as it flies overhead to check you out. As with all mimicry, don't overdo it. One call in response to a bird you hear should be sufficient to bring it close to you.

All observation or photography at or near a nest site must be done under licence from the relevant authority.

Many barn owls are of a nervous disposition around the nest site and visits must be kept to an absolute minimum if there is any risk that a

Egg laying: 1–2 broods from mid-March (later in colder springs)

Clutch size: 4–6 eggs

Incubation: 31–32 days (incubation starts after first egg is laid so hatching takes place over 10 days or so)

Fledging: 56–60 days

sitting bird may be flushed. Once the chicks have hatched there is a little more leeway in the tolerance of the parent birds, but even then, extreme caution should be deployed so as not to disturb them. Portable or more permanent hides are a must with all nest photography, and be sure to pay attention to the amount of noise made within the hide. Barn owls react adversely to even the smallest sounds. A DSLR camera mirror clacking at close quarters certainly gains their attention and may make them nervous. Human voices startle them too.

I once filmed a nesting pair in a roof from behind a thick plywood partition and I was working through optically perfect glass to further dampen any sound. As I watched the female incubating, I was able to establish her reaction to certain sounds and was astonished at just how acute her hearing was, and how nervous she could become at the merest hint of an approaching human. This was in the days of film cameras and, though very quiet, my Arriflex camera produced a faint whirring sound when it was running. Despite the plywood and glass, I had to cover the camera in thick padding to stifle all sounds that could come from it so as not to startle the sitting bird.

Exterior views of birds coming and going from nest sites must also be conducted under licence since the observer is still technically at the nest site. Here again, hides are a must, as is complete silence. All the usual hide deployment strategies should be observed (page 24).

Barn owls spend a lot of time hunting from perches, particularly on very dark nights. A well-used perch (often by a low branch or perhaps a fence post) may show signs of activity, with droppings and even pellets nearby or beneath it. While observation of such hunting behaviour is very challenging, night-viewing equipment (page 9) can provide a window on this world. If a well-used perch is identified it also opens up the possibility of flash photography, either with a manned camera from a hide, or using a remote camera trap system.

TAWNY OWL *Strix aluco*

SIGN

NEST

Tawny owls usually nest in cavities in trees, but will also raise a family in rocky hollows and in holes in buildings – especially older-style chimneys. In some areas they adopt old birds' nests, such as those built by buzzard, magpie or sparrowhawk, and they may even nest between tree roots on the ground. They also take readily to nest boxes of various designs, as long as the entrance hole is sufficiently large (about 15cm diameter) and the box floor has a reasonably deep litter of wood chip or dry leaves on the floor.

Tawnys do not bring any nest material into the cavity, but they do scrape vigorously on the floor of a potential site before deciding whether or not it is suitable for egg laying. In boxes or any other nest or cavity where the floor is hard and flat with no litter, tawnys are unlikely to settle. Nest scraping is undertaken by both male and female and a rudimentary depression is created on the floor into which the eggs are laid. An occupied nest cavity shows no external sign that a tawny pair is in residence. Where cavities are shallow, it may be possible to glimpse the top of the female bird's head while she is incubating.

OTHER SIGN

Pellets are cast from roosting points and, from time to time, randomly from a perch such as a fence post during the night. Nesting females (who alone incubate the eggs and break up large prey for the chicks) cast within the nest cavity, but unlike barn owls, tawnys do not actively break up their own pellets to create a litter on the floor of the chamber. Roosting locations are very often in thick ivy or other cover, close to the trunk of a large tree or abandoned building, and several pellets may be found littering the ground beneath a well-used site.

Tawny pellets are cylindrical, longer than they are wide, measuring about 3cm by 2cm. They are usually grey in colour and rather bumpy on the exterior, with a few bone fragments showing on the outside. One end is often more

SIZE
Weight: M 420g; F 520g
Length: 37–39cm
Wingspan: 82–105cm

Tawny owl pellets are usually grey and bumpy, sausage shaped and rounded at both ends.

Tawny owls are strictly
nocturnal hunters, but
on rare occasions adults
do come out of their day
roosting site for a stretch.

tapered than the other. Contents usually include lots of mouse and vole remains, but this species is very catholic in its diet so anything from frog and bird remains to earthworm fragments may turn up.

Droppings are off-white, with a distinct yellow tinge. Well-used roost sites may have spatters of droppings on the vegetation beneath, but since this species almost always roosts outdoors, any rainfall effectively washes away all but the most recent droppings. As with many owl species, moulted feathers may be found beneath favoured roosting sites.

HOW TO WATCH

Though tawny owls are the most common owl in the region, they are almost exclusively nocturnal; opportunities to watch them are few, unless you have specialist night-viewing equipment.

Establishing that tawny owls are in an area is straightforward enough, since they are very vocal, with peaks of singing in the early autumn and again in the early spring. Owls may sing at almost any time of year, however, with both male and female producing the familiar 'whoooo... who, who, who, whooooooooo' song, though the male's voice is much louder and more pure than the croaky, quiet version of the song produced by his mate. She is much more likely to respond to his singing with a high pitched 'ke-wick' call. Duets of this nature almost certainly gave rise to the erroneous description of a tawny owl song as 'twit-twoooo'; the 'twit' being the female 'ke-wick', the 'twooo' the first part of the male's hooting song.

In the early build-up to nesting and while nest site prospecting, both male and female birds produce a low-intensity warbling call. Though this sound is low in volume, on a still night it carries a fair distance and is a sure sign of nesting activity.

Very occasionally, a male tawny owl starts singing while it is still light, and it may be possible to track the source of the sound for a good view of the bird. Tawnys respond readily to mimicry or playback of their call, and while this is an effective way of catching a glimpse of a bird, it must also be used with caution and restraint, as is the case with any mimicry. There are commercially available whistles which, when blown carefully, produce just the right tone and timbre of a male tawny voice. Alternatively, it is possible to mimic their call, either by blowing through your thumbs or producing a low whistle with your lips.

To solicit a response, go into a known territory at dusk or just before dawn. Stand with your back to a tree to break up your outline and produce a single song phrase. The key to success is timing, as well as the quality of your call. Listen to tawnys singing to get a feel for how long a gap should be left between each phrase; an 8–10 second interval is the norm. With luck, a curious territorial male will fly over you in search of the intruder and start to sing nearby. If you are tempted to use a spotlight to improve the view after dark, add a red filter to the lens so as not to blind the bird you are trying to observe. Once you have had a view, just wait, watch and listen as the voices of the night rise up around you.

Extreme caution should be adopted if you are considering looking for or visiting a tawny owl nest. Despite being rather

TAWNY OWL'S YEAR

Egg laying: 1 brood from mid-March (later in colder springs)

Clutch size: 2–3 eggs, laid every 2 days or so

Incubation: 30 days (incubation starts after first egg is laid so hatching takes place over a week or so)

Fledging: 35–40 days

Young tawny owls leave the nest before they can fly proficiently. They are adept at fluttering and clambering through the branches by night, and as they rest by day, may be more exposed than their more experienced parents.

common, widespread and frequently living within suburbia, tawny owls are very nervous when raising a family. Flushing a female bird from the nest cavity, especially during the early stages of incubation, can easily lead to desertion of the clutch. They are a little more resilient once the chicks have hatched, but even at this stage, any undue disturbance can lead to desertion. Confirming nesting success is best done later in the season once chicks are fledged, when they produce repetitive, wheezing hunger calls. I have observed and recorded the nesting behaviour of tawny owls, but have always achieved this by installing live network cameras in suitable nest sites well ahead of any likely nesting period.

Tawny owls do not appear to respond to the mimicry of the calls made by their prey and instead seem to hunt using visual cues alone. Therefore, mimicry of prey species is not an effective way of soliciting a response.

LITTLE OWL *Athene noctua*

SIGN

NEST

Little owls are hole nesters, choosing cavities in buildings, trees and sometimes rocky outcrops. There are records of nests in piles of wood, rabbit burrows and between bales of hay and peat stacks to name just a few.

Most commonly, these owls nest in the hollows of large hedgerow trees, at heights from close to ground level to about eight metres, or in roof spaces or other cavities of older buildings. They don't build a nest but simply occupy the cavity and scrape a shallow depression in the floor detritus in which the eggs are laid.

The owls will also use purpose-built nest boxes, with an entrance hole dimension of 7cm, but the design should include a tunnel within the box that allows internal access to a dark chamber. Nest boxes are best located in open-fronted outbuildings, though can be sited in trees.

OTHER SIGN

Pellets are small, 1.5–4cm long and 1.5cm wide, and may contain a mix of small mammal remains, birds and insects. Beetle elytra are commonly found in little owl pellets. Pellets are found below roosting sites in trees and buildings and below well-used hunting perches such as fence posts.

SIZE
Weight: 180g
Length: 23–27cm
Wingspan: 56cm

LITTLE OWL'S YEAR

Egg laying: 1 brood from mid-March (later in colder springs)

Clutch size: 3–5 eggs

Incubation: 24–25 days, often from first egg

Fledging: 25–27 days

Little owls are frequently active in broad daylight, their cryptic plumage helping them blend into their surroundings.

HOW TO WATCH

Little owls are crepuscular and at times diurnal, as well as having activity periods through the night. They often sit very close to their potential nest site for protracted periods early on in the season, giving a good indication of where to search later in the spring. They are also vociferous, calling with increased regularity as the breeding season approaches.

They respond well to mimicry of their long hoot call. Listen carefully to recordings of little owls hooting, paying close attention to the pause duration (usually about seven seconds). Practise your mimicry before attempting it in the field.

ALARM SIGN

Little owls elicit mobbing responses from a number of passerines and larger birds, though rarely with the same level of vigour as is displayed to a roosting tawny owl. Chaffinches especially will persist with their 'pink-pink' mobbing alarm, and blackbirds too will let you know if they have rumbled a little owl in its roost site.

In flight, they cause a ripple of alarm of medium to low intensity among surrounding passerines, but rarely excite corvids (other than magpies) to the point of mobbing.

SHORT-EARED OWL *Asio flammeus*

SIGN

NEST

This species is fully protected by law and you need a licence to observe it at the nest. It nests on the ground in a variety of habitats, but is usually associated with heathland and moorland with rough grasses. The nest itself is no more than a shallow scrape on the ground. The eggs are incubated by the female alone, who may sit very tight, so cold searching for a nest is rarely successful. Males with prey return directly to the nest and so are a good guide to location.

SIZE

Female larger than male
Weight: 205–475g
Length: 33–40cm
Wingspan: 95–105cm

SHORT-EARED OWL'S YEAR

Egg laying: 1–2 broods from mid-March (later in colder springs)

Clutch size: 4–7 eggs

Incubation: 24–28 days (incubation starts after first egg is laid so hatching takes place over 10 days or so)

Fledging: 26–30 days

This is the only truly diurnal owl in the region. It often quarters low over its grassland habitat in broad daylight, looking for voles.

SIZE
Female larger than male
Weight: 180–430g
Length: 31–40cm
Wingspan: 87–100cm

OTHER SIGN

Pellets are 3–6cm long, rounded in cross-section and cylindrical; they are rounded at one end, more tapered at the other and tend to be grey, compact, but not dense. They usually contain the skulls of small mammals (especially voles), small birds and other bone fragments bound with small mammal hair.

HOW TO WATCH

This is the only owl species besides barn owls that appears to use hearing as its primary sense to locate prey. It often hunts by day and observation techniques are similar to those used for barn owls. It will react to mimicry of a vole, especially at dusk or at first light (page 186).

LONG-EARED OWL *Asio otus*

This is a largely nocturnal owl which usually lives in forested country with access to open ground for hunting, and it is generally difficult to observe. Its pellets are 3–4cm long, narrow, twisted and elongate, and contain small mammal, bird and insect remains.

Long-eared owls breed in the disused nests of other birds, especially those of magpie, sparrowhawk and wood pigeon, and start very early in the year – eggs are laid from the beginning of February. They can be coaxed into the open with the use of mimicry from January through to early April. The hooting call of the male is uttered in a long series of repeats. Each hoot is a single syllable 'whoo' note and is forceful and resonant. Gaps between notes are two to four seconds long and the hoot may be repeated up to 200 times in a single session. It is relatively easy to reproduce the call with the human voice.

In winter, in areas where prey is plentiful, long-eared owls sometimes gather in large day roosts. This is especially true in continental Europe, where roosts of 100 or more birds may occur, but even in the UK communal roosts with 10 or 20 birds are not uncommon. Such roosting sites may be used for days or weeks if undisturbed, affording excellent views of the birds.

Newly fledged owl young may often be more visible and confiding than adult birds.

BUZZARD *Buteo buteo*

SIGN

NEST

The buzzard's nest is a substantial structure of sticks, usually built in the upper third of a mature tree, and is likely to be where two or more branches form a cup at the base into which the nest is wedged. It can appear surprisingly small from below, given the size of the bird that makes it, but most buzzard nests measure a metre or more across the top. Nests are also sometimes built on cliff ledges, rocky crags or even very low down in shrubby cover.

Fresh green material is added to the nest in the final stages of building, during egg laying, and in the early stages of raising chicks. More green may be added throughout the chick-rearing period and sprigs of green may be visible from below, poking over the edges of the nest, confirming that it is in active use. As chicks develop, the edge of the nest becomes littered with their white, fluffy down, which is also visible from the ground.

High aerial display flights early in the season (from late January or before on bright sunny days) indicate the rough area of a potential nest site. Birds soar, call and perform drop and rise rollercoaster flights in the airspace over the nesting territory. At the end of sky dancing displays, one or both birds may descend rapidly to the tree in which the nest will be built, or one very nearby, and as the season develops these displays culminate in mating. Once eggs are laid, the female may sit tight, or, more likely, slip off the nest if she hears a human approach. She and her mate will then fly around in an agitated fashion, calling frequently. Despite being a common raptor, buzzards are nervous birds, especially at the nest and so great care must be taken not to disturb them.

OTHER SIGN

Pellets are cast randomly around the territory. They tend to be long (up to about 8cm) and cylindrical, with the odd twist. Some may superficially resemble a fox scat, but the lack of strong scent from the pellet should prevent confusion. They can contain anything from bone fragments and the hair of small mammals to insect remains and soil (from earthworms).

SIZE
Female larger than male
Weight: 550g–1.3kg
Length: 48–58cm
Wingspan: 1.09–1.36m

One of the most widespread and visible raptors in the region, buzzards are nonetheless nervous birds. A careful approach is needed for close observation.

HOW TO WATCH

Buzzards are easy to observe when soaring and displaying. Newly fledged chicks draw attention to themselves with constant hunger calling, both from the perch and while flying. Several birds may feed close to each other in fields where invertebrate prey is readily available, such as in freshly cut meadows or tilled earth. These gatherings can be observed at close quarters, using a portable hide (page 24).

Buzzards are naturally cautious and have excellent eyesight. When observing them from a portable hide, use the maximum amount of scrim netting around the observation port to prevent them from seeing any of your movements within the hide. When filming buzzards at the nest from a hide on a 25 metre scaffold tower, I not only scrimmed the viewing port, but also camouflaged my hands and face to reduce the chance of being spotted by the adult birds. Even then, there were one or two occasions when I was under the impression I was being watched!

ALARM SIGN

Corvids, especially carrion crows, will mob a flying buzzard and draw attention to their pursuit with guttural mobbing calls. Other bird species are less enthusiastic to draw attention to a flying or perched buzzard, since it poses

little or no threat to most small passerines. Pheasants may give low intensity alarm calls when they are watching a perched buzzard, as may partridge. Squirrels (both grey and red) give anxiety calls at the sight of a perched bird and may draw attention to a buzzard which is sitting on a nest.

RED KITE *Milvus milvus*

Persecuted to the brink of extinction in the UK at the end of the 19th century, red kites have since make a good recovery, thanks largely to reintroduction schemes in various parts of the nation. There are now several good red kite feeding stations in England, Scotland and especially Wales, where they hung on as a breeding bird throughout. At these, kites flock, sometimes in their hundreds, to snatch a meal. A visit to one will provide spectacular views.

[OPPOSITE] Buzzards are opportunists and catholic feeders, taking carrion and hunting anything from rabbits and other small mammals to birds and many earthworms.

[RIGHT] Red kites are spectacular acrobats in the air, twisting and diving to snatch scraps of carrion. Unlike buzzards, they prefer to feed on the wing or from a tree perch and rarely spend much time on the ground.

PEREGRINE *Falco peregrinus*

SIGN

NEST

The peregrine nests on coastal or inland cliff ledges, usually in the upper third of any cliff face or quarry wall, but sometimes lower down. In urban areas it commonly uses ledges on high buildings, and takes readily to purpose-built nest platforms in this environment. It does not actually build a nest, but scrapes a shallow dish in the substrate, and the area around the nest becomes littered with cast pellets and the feathers of prey as the season wears on.

Guano smears below the nest ledge, and on any wall face next to the scrape, become very noticeable as chicks grow.

OTHER SIGN

Pellets may be found on ledges, roofs and below favoured roosting sites. They are 3–4cm long, oval and compact, comprising almost exclusively the feathers and bone fragments of birds. Well-used perches, roosting sites and nest ledges all become heavily soiled by guano, and though the 'whitewashing' is hard to identify specifically as the work of peregrines, in suitable habitats it is a good indicator of favoured spots.

Peregrines cache food, especially when raising a family. You are unlikely to come across a cache accidentally

SIZE

Weight: M up to 1kg; F up to 1.5kg
Length: M 38–45cm; F 46–51cm
Wingspan: M 89–100cm; F 1.04–1.13m

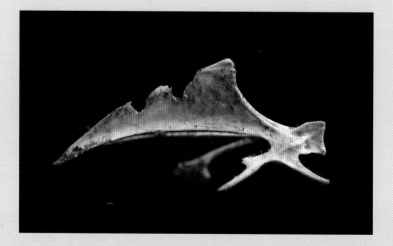

[LEFT] The sternum (breastbone) of a partridge, killed and eaten by a peregrine. Note the 'V'-shaped notches in the bone made by the raptor's powerful beak.

[RIGHT] Areas beneath favourite perches become coated with the peregrine's off-white guano. Such places can be eye-catching from a considerable distance.

(unless you are a climber or steeplejack), but at known nest sites out of the breeding season, a great deal can be learned about the peregrine's diet by sorting through prey remains. Caches are frequently on ledges 10–20 metres away from the nest ledge and may be in a covered cranny or, on buildings, tucked into gutters or other drainage routes.

In winter, kills are often eaten on the ground and these remains too are distinctive. The wings of birds eaten by a peregrine are usually left intact, often still connected to the body. The breast meat is eaten first and the sternum is likely to bear deep 'V' notches where the falcon's beak has broken through it. The head of the kill may or may not be removed.

HOW TO WATCH

As the fastest creature on earth, peregrines have been recorded diving (stooping) at well over 321kph. Their blistering turn of speed, hunting behaviour and dynamic, wide-ranging flight makes them one of the most exciting raptors to watch.

Urban pairs frequently stay on territory throughout the year, as do coastal birds. Those using inland quarries tend to range more widely outside the nesting season, though this depends a great deal on food availability.

Protracted vigils from vantage points that offer wide vistas in a peregrine's territory are usually fruitful. Peregrines are protected by law and any disturbance at the nest site can only be conducted under licence. If you are in a location where peregrines are nesting, be certain to keep a good distance between your viewing post and the nest. A disturbed peregrine will leave the nest ledge and may fly over to the observer, calling. If this should occur, beat a very hasty retreat!

There are many well-known peregrine nest sites up and down the country which can be observed using a telescope from a safe distance.

ALARM SIGN

As one of the most efficient bird predators in the world, peregrines cause significant alarm among a wide variety of bird species. Listen for high, reedy alarm calls from

PEREGRINE'S YEAR

Egg laying: 1 brood March/April

Clutch size: 2–4 eggs (usually 3)

Incubation: 31 days (incubation starts after second egg is laid)

Fledging: 30–32 days

A powerful flight on long, scythe-shaped wings gives the peregrine an imposing presence in the skies. Listen for the high, sibilant alarms from blackbirds and robins for a hint that a peregrine may be flying overhead.

blackbirds, robins and others. These lack the urgency of those produced in response to a sparrowhawk flying low and close, but nonetheless have a subdued 'fearful' character and tend to go on for longer in response to a high-flying peregrine. Swallows, house martins and other hirundines all give medium to strong intensity flight alarm calls and may group and fly synchronously in an open flock. Wader flocks rise and 'smoke', flying tightly and ascending rapidly. This is especially noticeable with flocks of lapwing and golden plover inland, and knot and dunlin on the coast. These 'smokes' will peel and split if the peregrine attacks, becoming a swirling amorphous 'shoal' of birds. If a peregrine flies low and fast over a water body, it may raise flocks of duck and other water fowl. Watch for flocks of wood pigeons rising from woodland and fields, a phenomenon which can ripple over a broad landscape and chart the movements of the predator even if you can't actually see it.

Starling flocks bunch and utter their high, metallic alarm calls, in much the same way as they do when they react to a low passing or soaring sparrowhawk, but with even more urgency to their flight and tighter formation. Large roosting flocks of starlings are at their most spectacular when a peregrine appears on the scene, since the presence of the falcon precipitates the most dramatic formation shifts and swirls, the flock cleaving open as the falcon sweeps through its centre.

Few birds risk mobbing a peregrine in flight, exceptions being ravens and other raptors. Some other corvids, especially carrion crows, may try to hassle a flying hawk but they run the very real risk of becoming a meal in the process. I have witnessed a large flock of jackdaws mobbing a peregrine which had just snatched a newly fledged chick from the midst of a colony nesting in a quarry. They succeeded in causing the hawk to drop its victim, which then flew away.

In urban settings, watch for sudden 'panicked' flights of pigeons flying from rooftops and dropping low between buildings. Where gulls nest in cities, both herring and lesser black-backed gulls produce loud alarm calls at the sight of a peregrine, circling high and keeping a wary eye on the hawk.

KESTREL *Falco tinnunculus*

SIGN

NEST

Prior to settling on a nest site, male and female kestrels display around likely breeding territories. This takes the form of low to medium height flights past potential nesting locations, accompanied by loud calling. A male may make 'winnowing' flight displays, when he beats his wings in a shallow flutter, then dips and twists through the air from time to time, again while calling. Both sexes visit nest sites repeatedly and call from them, sometimes nest scraping by forcing their chest into the floor of the site and kicking back with their talons.

Like most falcons, kestrels do not build a nest structure as such, but instead lay their eggs in the abandoned nests of other species, such as crows, or in any shallow scrape that is protected from the worst of the weather. Many nests are in tree cavities, while others are in buildings where holes or ledges provide a suitable platform. Kestrels take readily to suitable nest boxes, either with open fronts or entrance holes at least 15cm in diameter.

SIZE
Weight: M 190g; F 220g
Length: 34cm
Wingspan: 76cm

KESTREL'S YEAR
Egg laying: 1 brood from mid-April (later in colder springs)

Clutch size: 4–5 eggs

Incubation: 28–29 days

Fledging: 32–37 days

OTHER SIGN

Kestrel pellets are cast wherever the birds are resting and feel the urge to regurgitate. This may be from a favoured hunting perch, and small litters of kestrel pellets may be found on the ground beneath such sites. Late in the nesting season, as chicks start to inspect the world outside their nest, litters of pellets may collect beneath a nest ledge or hole. Pellets usually contain the hair of small mammals, bone fragments (though not whole skulls) and sometimes the remains of reptiles and insects.

HOW TO WATCH

Kestrels are conspicuous due to their hover-hunting technique and few special watching methods apply to this species. Excellent views can be had where kestrels hunt on steeply sloping ground, such as coastal paths and moorland hillsides, since in these landscapes it may be possible to sit on a level with or slightly above a hunting bird.

Kestrel pellets are about 3cm long and often tapered to more of a point on one end than the other. They commonly contain mammal hair and bones, insect remains, feathers and lizard scales.

ALARM SIGN

Kestrels sometimes target young birds but are ill equipped to outmanoeuvre fit adult birds in the air. As a result, the predator response from passerines, hirundines or other small birds to kestrels is usually of very low intensity or absent. When kestrels leave a perch they may elicit predator call responses from members of the tit family, and corvids will mob them both in the air and when they are perched.

HOBBY *Falco subbuteo*

SIGN

NEST
The hobby uses the old nests of other species, especially crows but also of jays and wood pigeons, and will even take over disused squirrel dreys.

This is a rare bird and is fully protected by law. Any deliberate searching for nests must be done under licence.

OTHER SIGN
Hobbies leave few signs, rarely using regular plucking posts. Pellets are scattered beneath any resting place, though may be concentrated in roost sites or near nests. They are distinctive – rounded, blackish in colour and loosely formed, comprising almost exclusively insect remains.

HOW TO WATCH
This is a fast-moving hunter. Hobbies can outmanoeuvre birds as aerobatic as swallows, martins and swifts, and while they hunt small birds when raising a family, the majority of

SIZE
Female up to 10 per cent larger than male
Weight: 131–340g
Length: 30–36cm
Wingspan: 82–92cm

HOBBY'S YEAR
Egg laying: 1 brood from mid-June
Clutch size: 3 eggs
Incubation: 28 days (incubation starts after first egg is laid)
Fledging: 28–32 days

Scythe-shaped wings and fluid, powerful flight are the hallmarks of an airborne hobby – one of the most dashing and acrobatic of raptors.

their prey is flying insects – especially dragonflies. In suitable wetland habitats, it is possible to watch several hobbies hunting in the same airspace, and the views can be breathtaking.

Choose a period of settled warm weather for your observations. Having established a regularly used hunting area, pay attention to the wind direction. Set up your viewing point with the wind behind you, since the hobbies are likely to fly into the wind when attacking their insect prey. Use available cover such as trees and bushes and, if necessary, augment this with scrim or a field hide (page 24).

Birds are likely to start hunting mid-morning, when dragonflies and damselflies take to the wing. Rapid flight, a mercurial character and feeding on the wing define this species and make it among the most exciting to watch.

ALARM SIGN

All birds make vigorous alarm calls at the sight of an approaching hobby, but none more so than the hirundines. Swallows shout loud alarm and frequently group together, flying rapidly away from the approaching falcon in a wave of birds. House martins have a loud lilting whistle that tells of a hobby's approach, a call so distinctive that it informs even the trained human ear. Sand martins similarly let the world know that a hobby is nearby, with loud scraping alarm calls.

When a hobby is bird hunting, it moves very swiftly and will be among a flock of martins or swallows seconds after the first alarm is raised. High aerial pursuits may follow, and, when newly fledged birds are in the groups of swallows or martins, these are often targeted, grabbed in mid-air and carried off. Plucking often starts while the hobby is still flying, and feather trails may be seen pouring from the sky. The remaining flock is likely to be streaming away in the opposite direction.

Other bird alarm calls are much the same as those produced when a sparrowhawk is in the vicinity, with members of the tit family producing high, sibilant calls, and robins and blackbirds emitting high, reedy whistles.

GOLDEN EAGLE *Aquila chrysaetos*

There are few methods besides observation in suitable habitats that can be used for watching golden eagles. These large, majestic birds are wary of close contact with humans and they are the true spirit of wilderness.

Nests are built of sticks and green vegetation and are usually on inaccessible crags and cliffs or in remote pines or birch trees in steep glens. Nest structures are huge, sometimes three metres or more across, and may have been added to by generations of eagles. Traditional nest sites are used year after year, the pair choosing from two or three (sometimes more) established locations. Pairs in the UK often stay on territory throughout the year and may display at any time of year in good weather. Both male and female 'sky-dance'. They soar high over the territory, then plummet on folded wings towards the earth before flaring and rising again. Display flights may end with one or both birds settling near the prospective nest site.

Golden eagles are very nervous near the nest and readily desert during the laying and incubation stages. They are fully protected by law and it is an offence to disturb them at the nest without a licence. Any observation should be conducted at a great distance through a telescope.

Golden eagles will feed on carrion, especially during autumn, winter and early spring. Close observation of the birds at a carcass can only be conducted with the use of a hide, and this must be introduced well in advance of any protracted wait.

Pellets may be found below well-used roost sites. They are huge – about 9–10cm long – compact and rounded at both ends. They usually contain mammal hair but very few bone fragments, unless the eagles have been hunting birds, when feathers and bone shards will be present.

SIZE

Female up to 20 per cent heavier and 10 per cent larger than male
Weight: 3–6kg
Length: 75–85cm
Wingspan: 2–2.2m

GOLDEN EAGLE'S YEAR

Egg laying: 1 brood from mid-March (later in colder springs)

Clutch size: 2 eggs

Incubation: starts with first egg, 43–45 days per egg

Fledging: 65–70 days

Both golden eagles [RIGHT] and sea eagles [FAR RIGHT] cut imposing figures in the skies. The scale of their enormous wingspan is often very hard to judge when they are flying at altitude over the open mountain and coastal habitats they prefer.

SIZE
Female up to 25 per cent heavier
and 15 per cent larger than male
Weight: 4–6.5kg
Length: 70–90cm
Wingspan: 2–2.4m

SEA EAGLE'S YEAR
Egg laying: 1 brood from mid-
March (later in colder springs)
Clutch size: 2–3 eggs
Incubation: starts with first egg,
38 days per egg
Fledging: 70–77 days

SEA EAGLE *Haliaeetus albicilla*

This huge raptor is hard to miss when it is soaring in the
open sky. It has a marked effect on other large birds such
as flocks of geese, which rise up in panic at the sight of
a sea eagle prospecting for a meal.

In some areas, sea eagles follow fishing boats and feed
on fish scraps thrown overboard. This habit has led to a
few pairs in the UK (and many in Norway and elsewhere
in northern Europe) becoming well habituated to humans,
thus allowing spectacular views.

Sea eagles readily come to carrion and once familiar
with a feeding station, they will accept an established hide.

Pellets are sometimes found beneath tree roosts. They
are large (9–11cm long), rounded at both ends and tend to
be rather flattened. They may contain anything from fish
remains to fur, feathers or sheep's wool.

SPARROWHAWK *Accipiter nisus*

SIGN

NEST

The sparrowhawk is a woodland species and closely associated with trees while raising a family.

Early in the season, both male and female indulge in display flights high over the prospective nesting territory, using slow deliberate wingbeats. Once nest building starts, most of these high displays come to an end and both birds become secretive and inconspicuous.

Sparrowhawks build a loose structure of twigs close to the trunk of a conifer where two or more branches provide a starting point for the platform; this is usually at heights of over four metres but sometimes lower. It may look like a wood pigeon nest, but the structure is bulkier and green material may be used to line the nest once building is almost complete.

A nest with reasonably large chicks will have guano streaks on the surrounding vegetation and on the ground below, and white downy feathers are likely to show around the edge of the nest when viewed from below. Some nests are built in deciduous trees such as oak, ash or birch, where two or more branches form a cup. I have found nests low in spindly young trees such as rowan, but sites such as these are very rare.

SIZE
Weight: M 110–196g; F 185–342g
Length: M 29–34cm; F 35–41cm
Wingspan: M 58–65cm; F 67–80cm

OTHER SIGN

Throughout the nesting period, male sparrowhawks bring prey to their mates. While they may do this at the nest platform, they are more likely to establish a plucking post within 50 metres or so of the nest site. Here they prepare the meal by plucking it and the female comes to take her meal once the male calls to her with a high, rapid chittering.

Plucking posts are usually in woodland, half a metre to two metres off the ground, on a fallen tree or tree stump. A litter of feathers from many different bird species, strewn over the top of the post and on the ground below, is distinctive, and could only be confused with the plucking post of another raptor like a goshawk. The post of the latter, however, is likely to include the remains of larger species and some mammals such as squirrels or rabbits.

Feathers of birds killed and eaten by a sparrowhawk retain the quill tip intact, as it is plucked, rather than chewed, from the prey.

Prey is plucked before being eaten. Small birds such as redwing are often taken to low branches to be plucked [ABOVE LEFT], whereas larger prey, such as wood pigeons, are often plucked on the ground [ABOVE RIGHT].

Away from the breeding site, sparrowhawks leave sign of their kills typical of most raptors that target birds. The primary and secondary wing feathers, if plucked from the wing, have the point of the quill intact, not chewed (see Stoat page 62 and Red fox page 28) and show little or no damage where the raptor's beak has gripped the feather before plucking. Sometimes the majority of wing feathers are left in place; only the breast feathers are plucked before the sparrowhawk begins to feed, and these will be scattered in a circle or downwind of the feeding site. Sparrowhawks often start plucking their prey long before it is dead, and the resulting litter of feathers may be scattered over a significant area, with two or three 'hot spots' as the hawk gets to grips with its struggling quarry. This is especially true with larger prey species such as pigeons and corvids.

The breastbone of a bird that has been consumed by a raptor is likely to bear 'V' shaped notches in it made by the killer's beak, and the size and depth of these notches is a guide to the species concerned. Sparrowhawks leave narrow notches in the breastbone of smaller bird species, but few or no marks on the sternum of larger species (see Peregrine page 200 for comparison).

HOW TO WATCH

A true avian hunter, sparrowhawks can tackle other bird species up to the size of a large pigeon. Male sparrowhawks are significantly smaller than females and tend to target smaller prey. They adopt at least three distinct hunting techniques: the search and drop, low-level surprise, and perch hunting. The first two are both conducted at speed and on the wing.

When search and drop hunting a bird gains height and finds a thermal before circling high over a hunting ground. From this vantage point, the sparrowhawk spots its target, perhaps a group of house sparrows feeding in a garden. The start of the attack usually occurs a significant distance away from where the raptor intends to end up, using the advantage of distance and speed to spring a sudden ambush on its quarry. Once committed, the hawk drops rapidly, often at an acute angle, pulling its wings close to its body and occasionally power-thrusting to increase its speed. Most hunts of this nature go out of the observer's line of sight, but on several occasions I have witnessed the conclusion. On some of these, the sparrowhawk levelled out its flight close to the ground and used physical objects such as hedges and buildings to conceal its approach. It then burst into the spot where its intended targets were feeding, oblivious of the approaching raptor. Often, a kill is not made immediately but instead birds scatter into nearby cover, where the sparrowhawk sits, peering in and attempting to grab a meal with its extraordinarily far-reaching legs and talons.

Low-level surprise hunting, often referred to as hedge-hopping, is a more haphazard version of the final stages of the search and drop hunt. The raptor flies low and fast through its territory, using every feature in the environment to camouflage its approach, then reacts suddenly and with deadly accuracy to any suitable quarry it surprises. Sparrowhawks may repeatedly visit locations where they have been successful in the past, and busy bird feeding stations are favourites for this.

When perch hunting the hawk watches from a more or less concealed perch for other birds, or sometimes small mammals, then dashes out to grab a meal. I have witnessed this at bird feeding stations and also where other birds are nesting. The hawk may take chicks from the nests of many species, including blackbirds and swallows.

SPARROWHAWK'S YEAR

Egg laying: 1 brood from late April (later in colder springs)

Clutch size: 5–6 eggs

Incubation: 32–36 days (incubation starts after second or third egg)

Fledging: 26–28 days

Sparrowhawks are mercurial hunters of other birds and encounters with them in the field are often very fleeting. Some of the most protracted views occur when these hawks target a meal in your own back garden.

ALARM SIGN

If spotted by other birds, sparrowhawks elicit very strong predator alarm call responses. Blue and great tits use sibilant, piercingly high-pitched calls; long-tailed tits emit high tremulous alarm calls. Blackbirds and robins also use high, reedy alarm notes when watching a flying sparrowhawk. Swallows and house martins make high anxiety alarm notes. The movement of a flying sparrowhawk can be tracked through a woodland or other cover by the ripple of alarm caused ahead of its arrival, and in its wake. Starling flocks rise and spiral, bunching tightly and uttering metallic alarm calls.

A perched sparrowhawk may cause neighbouring birds to produce more traditional mobbing calls, such as the 'pink-pink-pink' of the blackbird, or the rattling of a wren, but the moment the hawk takes to the wing, high-pitched sibilant alarms sound, as the avian community responds to the imminent aerial threat.

GOSHAWK *Accipiter gentilis*

Goshawks are birds of forest and shadows. Despite their size, they keep a low profile and can be very tricky to see, even in areas where they are fairly common. Their nests are like those of their close cousin, the sparrowhawk, but super-sized. They are usually built in trees, especially in pines and beech, but also in other large deciduous species.

In early spring, the male or pair may display flight over nesting territory, soaring with tail coverts fanned, then circling with very slow deliberate wing beats and performing a diving 'skydance'.

Once nest building is underway both birds are very vocal, especially just before dawn. The female spends a great deal of time calling, while her mate collects nesting material, answering her as he arrives at the nest site. These screeches and whistles carry through the forest and are a great clue to the birds' whereabouts.

Goshawk pellets are similar to those of sparrowhawks but larger, measuring 3–5cm. Rounded at one end and tapered at the other, they contain feathers and fur, but very little bone.

Males use a regular plucking post to prepare meals before bringing them to the nest. (See Sparrowhawk page 210 for details of observation at the plucking post.)

OSPREY *Pandion haliaetus*

Ospreys are nervous birds at the nest and protected by law. Any observation close to breeding birds which could cause disturbance must be done under licence only.

Hunting is exclusively over water, targeting fish. Most hunting ospreys fly at a reasonable height of 30 metres or higher, patrolling at a fair pace while watching the water below. At the hint of a fish the osprey may check its flight and plummet headlong to the water, pulling its head back and thrusting its talons forward at the last split second before impact. Sometimes it may hover to scrutinise the water more carefully before dropping.

In some locations, such as fish farms, ospreys predictably hunt in a relatively small area, providing excellent close views. There are one or two facilities in the UK that provide photographers and enthusiasts with views of wild hunting ospreys, which have learned to visit specially stocked pools. Ospreys almost invariably face into the wind when they make their strike, and when they lift from the water with their fish kill. Ensure the wind is behind you when settling to watch in a known hunting zone to ensure face-on views of the birds.

Ospreys patrolling inland waters rarely provoke any predator response from smaller birds, but flocks of gulls lift up as an osprey passes overhead. This is odd behaviour, since an osprey will not target any prey other than fish.

SIZE
Female a little larger than male
Weight: 1.4kg
Length: 56–60cm
Wingspan: 1.47–1.66m

OSPREY'S YEAR
Egg laying: 1 brood in April (soon after return to UK from African wintering grounds
Clutch size: 2–4 eggs, usually 3
Incubation: starts with first or second egg, 32–38 days per egg
Fledging: 52–53 days

[LEFT AND OPPOSITE] Ospreys are consummate hunters, targeting their fish prey with precision and achieving a remarkably high success rate. Few sights in nature are as dramatic.

HARRIERS

SIGN

NEST

Hen, marsh and Montagu's harriers are ground-nesting birds. In the UK each species occupies different habitats and niches. Marsh harriers generally choose to nest in areas of extensive reed beds, while hen harriers nest in heathland, upland moors and young forestry plantations. Montagu's harriers in the UK tend to use fields of arable crops. All are sensitive at the nest site and are fully protected by law.

HOW TO WATCH

Early in the year, watch for noisy display flights of all three species, with lots of aerial chasing between pairs, food passing from the male to the female, and nest building.

Harriers have low wing loading in flight. This means that they can maintain a slow ground speed without falling out of the sky. Typically, all hunting harriers fly low and slow, scouring the ground below for a meal. They stop suddenly when they spot something and drop on to it, or sometimes flush small birds and engage in a short chase.

If watching hunting harriers, try to position yourself with the wind behind you to maximise head-on views of the birds as they hawk into the wind. The more you camouflage your outline, the more likely you are to enjoy very close views.

Montagu's *Circus pygargus*
Length: 43–47cm;
Wingspan: 105–120cm

Hen *Circus cyaneus*
Length: 41–52cm;
Wingspan: 97–122cm

Marsh *Circus aeruginosus*
Length: 48–56cm;
Wingspan: 115–130cm

HARRIER'S YEAR

All three species in UK follow a similar calendar

Egg laying: 1 clutch in early May

Clutch size: 4 or 5 eggs

Incubation: about 30 days (35 for marsh harrier)

Fledging: about 40 days

As with other harrier species, the marsh harrier's long broad wings and low body weight allow it to fly low and slow in search of prey.

NIGHTJAR *Caprimulgus europaeus*

SIGN

NEST

Nightjars nest on the ground in open heathland, bracken patches and areas of clear-felled forestry. They lay their eggs in a shallow scrape and avoid detection by virtue of their astonishing cryptic camouflage. A sitting bird is unlikely to flush from the nest until the very last moment, making detection very difficult. Watching at dusk may reveal both male or female flying low and briefly hovering before dropping on to the ground, giving a guide to the whereabouts of the nest. Nightjars are tight sitters, but once discovered can be very nervous. Extreme caution should be exercised in the vicinity of a nest and any disturbance kept to an absolute minimum.

HOW TO WATCH

Nightjars leave virtually no sign in the field. They do, however, make themselves heard at dusk, dawn and from time to time throughout the night with the male's churring song and display flights. Mimicry of nightjar calls is extremely difficult without using playback, and this can only be done with a licence from the relevant bodies. The birds react strongly to the playback recording, but a high-quality speaker is a must to ensure that the full range of frequencies is broadcast.

Male nightjars have white flashes on their wings and tail and these are highly visible at dusk as the birds execute their wing-clapping display flights. There are accounts of nightjars coming close to an observer waving white hankies, one in each hand. The idea is that a male nightjar reacts to the flashes of white, seeing them as a super-stimulus. Having tried this, I believe that while a male nightjar may fly close to someone waving white hankies, he is just as likely to fly close to an observer standing still in open heath. While they are shy birds by day, nightjars become much bolder, even inquisitive, at dusk and through the night and so may fly around you several times for a closer look.

SIZE
Weight: 50–100g
Length: 25–28cm
Wingspan: 52–59cm

NIGHTJAR'S YEAR
Arrives in Europe from African wintering grounds in April
Egg laying: 2 broods in May
Clutch size: 2 eggs
Incubation: 18 days
Fledging: about 18 days

Nests are nothing more than a scrape on the ground. Nightjars rely on their superb camouflage to avoid detection.

GREEN WOODPECKER *Picus viridis*

SIGN

NEST

This species is much more vociferous than the more common great spotted woodpecker, and its loud laughing call carries a good distance through woodland and across fields. There are reliable accounts of green woodpeckers drumming, but in over 50 years in the field I have never witnessed it first hand, so it is safe to assume that it occurs rarely. They rely more on their voice than on a ritualised hammering on a tree to proclaim territorial rights (see Great spotted woodpecker page 220).

The bird drills a nest hole into the trunk of a tree using its powerful beak. New nest holes are bored most years, though old holes may be reused, as may large nest boxes with wood chips on the floor. The diameter of the entrance is about 7cm.

Most holes are made in the main trunk of a dead tree, 3–12 metres above ground level, sometimes lower. Live trees with dead heartwood may also be used.

It may be possible to find a nest at the excavation stage by looking for fresh wood chips on the ground beneath suitable sites. Carefully listening for boring activity may narrow down a search area.

Once incubation has started, birds are hard to locate. If a nest hole is spotted, it may be possible to flush a sitting bird by scraping the base of the tree and mimicking the sound made by the claws of a predator like a pine marten, though many birds sit tight and may not flush unless the tree is climbed.

Once the chicks hatch they are tended by both parents, and as they grow become increasingly noisy. During the last week they are in the nest, they regularly stick their heads out of the nest hole and call, drawing attention to themselves.

OTHER SIGN

This species feeds almost exclusively on ants and their eggs and larvae. Some grubs of wood-boring insects are taken, but green woodpeckers have evolved to feed on the ground, right down to their striking colouring which blends beautifully with the short-grass environment of many ant colonies. Ant nests that have been plundered will have much of the soil pecked

SIZE
Weight: 190g
Length: 35cm
Wingspan: 50cm

GREEN WOODPECKER'S YEAR

Egg laying: 1 brood from early April

Clutch size: 5–7 eggs

Incubation: 18–19 days

Fledging: 18–21 days

Green woodpeckers favour feeding on ants on the ground. Their plumage blends well with the surrounding vegetation.

away. Close inspection will reveal multiple rounded holes where the bird has pushed its beak into the nest before extending its long barbed tongue into the colony to scoop up its prey.

Droppings are characteristically cylindrical, shrouded in a greyish membrane and comprise compressed insect chitin, almost exclusively ant remains. These are often found on or around ant nests that have been attacked.

HOW TO WATCH

Since they are vulnerable when feeding on the ground, green woodpeckers tend to be jumpy birds that will take off and wait in a nearby tree for a human to pass by before flying back to earth and resuming feeding.

They are regular visitors to the lawns of large gardens and may be watched from the window of a house. In wilder settings, even where they see humans on a regular basis, they tend to be flighty, so the use of a hide in a favoured feeding area will yield the best views.

Great care must be taken when watching this species near the nest and use of a hide is essential to avoid disturbance.

GREAT SPOTTED WOODPECKER
Dendrocopos major

SIGN
NEST

The bird drills a nest hole into the trunk of a tree using its powerful beak. Nest locations are as for the green woodpecker (page 218). It may be possible to find a nest at the excavation stage by looking for fresh wood chips on the ground beneath suitable sites. Carefully listening for boring activity (much heavier blows and more sporadic rhythm than the drumming 'song' delivered by both male and female woodpeckers from February to early June) may narrow down a search area. Once incubation has started, birds are hard to locate. If a nest hole is spotted, it may be possible to flush a sitting bird by scraping the base of the tree, mimicking the sound made by the claws of a predator such as a pine marten, though many birds sit tight and may not flush unless the tree is climbed.

Once the chicks hatch they are tended by both parents, and as they grow become increasingly noisy. During the last week in the nest, they regularly stick their heads out of the nest hole and call, drawing attention to themselves.

When adults are feeding chicks they will alarm call if they spot a perceived danger close to the nest tree (this includes an unwitting human), and will hop around in adjacent trees, beaks full of grubs or other food, calling vigorously. The observer should retire to a distance which allows the bird to return to the nest, watching for the nest hole.

OTHER SIGN

The feeding activity of this species can leave lots of visible sign. Normal searching for beetle grubs in dead or dying wood leads to sections of bark and rotting wood being pried from the tree and cast on the floor beneath. Both the damage to the tree and the litter beneath are eye-catching.

Great spotted woodpeckers regularly feed on nuts and pine seeds. They often take pine cones to a favoured feeding site, such as an old rotting tree stump, and wedge them into fissures so that they can prise the scales away to reach the seeds beneath. A pine cone dealt with in this way will have

SIZE
Weight: 85g
Length: 25cm
Wingspan: 40cm

GREAT SPOTTED WOODPECKER'S YEAR
Drumming from February–June

Egg laying: 1 brood from early April

Clutch size: 4–7 eggs

Incubation: 16 days

Fledging: 18–21 days

Both male [ABOVE] and female great spotted woodpeckers feed the young in the nest.

its scales twisted and torn, some of which will have been roughly pulled from the axis and litter the ground in the surrounding area. Very well-used sites will have a number of spent cones on the floor, and others still stuck in the fissures of the stump. Hazelnuts and cob nuts may be dealt with in a similar way, the woodpecker finding a suitable point in which to wedge the nut before roughly breaking into it and extracting the kernel.

Great spotted woodpeckers raid other birds' nests from time to time. It is this species that is most likely to break into a wooden nest box to reach the eggs or chicks of species such as blue and great tits.

HOW TO WATCH

This species commonly visits gardens and may become a regular at bird feeding stations, showing a preference for peanuts and fat. Pairs draw attention to themselves early in the year when they start proclaiming their right to a territory by drumming. Both male and female drum, choosing a resonant tree trunk or branch (sometimes a telegraph post or even the metal work on pylons) and delivering 10–12 blows in under a second. I have found it impossible to mimic this sound in the field, but territorial birds will check out any suggestion that an invading woodpecker is in their home patch, even one that is feeding.

It is possible to mimic the sounds made by a feeding woodpecker by striking a stone against a resonant tree trunk or branch. If you are within a territory (you will have heard drumming, or heard a bird calling) start tapping sporadically, copying the actions of a feeding bird. Make sure you leave long gaps between bouts of tapping. If you are heard by the resident birds, one or both of them is likely to fly over to the tree you are tapping for a closer look. Keep your body close to the tree and movements to a minimum and with luck you will be rewarded with great views.

This species can be confiding or jumpy at the nest, depending on an individual's experiences with humans. It is always best to use a hide for observation and photography, but introduction of any structure can usually be conducted fairly swiftly – over a period of hours rather than days.

BITTERN *Botaurus stellaris*

Bitterns are remarkably well camouflaged in the reed bed environment they inhabit. In winter they are silent, so give no audible clue as to their whereabouts. Scour the edge of reed beds with your binoculars, looking for solid, dense patches of reed that may turn out to be a bittern standing stock still on the margins. Look out for clumps of reeds pinched together to form a sort of 'wigwam', then study the point where the reeds converge. This may be the work of a bittern using the reeds as a resting place by collecting a number of them in its feet and pinching them together for stability. In spring, the booming call of the male bittern betrays its presence. In occupied territories watch for the occasional flight as both male and female fly from one patch of reeds to the next.

Bitterns sometimes target starling roosts in reed beds, waiting for the flocks to alight in the reeds before flying into the centre of the mass to snatch a meal. If watching such a roost, study the area where the birds are settling as the last hint of light seeps from the sky. This is when the bitterns make their move.

SIZE
Weight: 865g–1.94kg
Length: 70–80cm
Wingspan: 1–1.3m

BITTERN'S YEAR

Egg laying: 1 brood from late March

Clutch size: 4–6 eggs

Incubation: 25 days

Fledging: about 8 weeks

Bitterns usually keep to the base of reeds, but on occasion they may climb the stalks and form a 'wigwam' structure for stability, holding the stems together with their long toes.

GREAT CRESTED GREBE *Podiceps cristatus*

This species performs complex and very beautiful courtship displays that are a joy to watch. Most display takes place within 100 metres or so of the nesting site, on the great crested grebe's favoured habitats of lowland open still or slow-moving water. It involves bouts of synchronised head shaking, pseudo-preening, and many other ritualised behaviours, including the weed dance. In this, both male and female dive to collect a beak full of aquatic weed, then come together and rise up, breast to breast, shaking their prize to and fro. Use a standard sit-and-wait tactic on the banks of a suitable freshwater habitat. Where necessary, camouflage and/or a hide can ensure closer views of the birds.

Grebes have a complex repertoire of calls, many associated with communication between a courting pair. One, which I call the honk-growl, is used in aggressive territorial encounters or the proclamation of territory ownership and this, if mimicked, will bring a grebe close to check out the competition. I make it using the falsetto range of my voice, and add a growling quality in my throat.

SIZE
Weight: 900g–1.5kg
Length: 45–60cm
Wingspan: 60–73cm

GREAT CRESTED GREBE'S YEAR

Egg laying: 1, sometimes 2 broods from late March

Clutch size: 3–5 eggs

Incubation: 27–29 days

Fledging: 9–10 weeks

Adopt a low profile or hidden viewing position for the closest views of grebes. Some urban lakes and ponds have well habituated grebes nesting on them, giving good views of this showy bird.

DIPPER *Cinclus cinclus*

SIGN

NEST

The dipper builds a domed nest of moss and grass that resembles an oversized wren's nest. It's usually made in a natural feature or man-made structure over fast-moving water – in the UK typically under bridges or in ducts and culverts. The nest may also be in a branch overhanging water and, exceptionally, in flood debris, such as plastic bags that have created a 'hammock' in overhanging vegetation. Dippers also use open-fronted nest boxes sited under suitable structures over moving water.

Early in the season, the male sings from vantage points all along his territory, and may concentrate his efforts close to a potential nest site. Once building starts, the birds are relatively easy to watch along their linear territory of a stream or river. Sit concealed on the bank and watch the direction of travel, as the birds go back and forth with beaks full of moss or grass.

Dippers are much harder to find once incubation starts because females sit very tight for protracted periods. Once the feeding of young begins, they are again quite easy to watch. Follow birds with beaks full of food through successive watching points along stream or river borders.

SIZE
Weight: 64g
Length: 17–20cm
Wingspan: 28cm

Despite their near-constant bobbing movement, dippers can be tricky to spot in the shadows of a stream. Listen for their 'zipping' flight call.

DIPPER'S YEAR

Egg laying: 1 or 2 broods from end of February

Clutch size: 4–6 eggs

Incubation: 16 days

Fledging: 19–25 days

OTHER SIGN

You are most unlikely to find a dipper pellet since almost all are cast into the water. Droppings, on the other hand, are good indicators of an occupied territory. Look for small, vividly white splashes on rocks in the centre of fast-moving streams. Close inspection will reveal a waxy quality.

HOW TO WATCH

Like kingfishers, dippers let you know they are coming with their piercing, abrasive call 'zzzit – zzzzit', and often all you see is a dark, dumpy bird on whirring wings flashing past you at speed, just a few centimetres above the water's surface. Dippers return time and again to favourite hunting areas. These are usually stretches of fast-moving shallow water, but dippers can and do swim on still open water. Using their wings as oars, they also duck dive to forage near the bottom or through vegetation. This behaviour tends to occur when their usual feeding places are affected by flood or drought.

These are tolerant little birds, and a quiet, still vigil often yields good views. Use of a portable hide is very effective and even covering your outline with bracken or large tufts of grass will help give you great views if you wait in an appropriate spot.

[ABOVE LEFT] A typical dipper stream, with fairly fast-moving water and plenty of rocks and shadows.

[ABOVE RIGHT] Close inspection of rocks mid-stream may reveal the dipper's white waxy droppings.

KINGFISHER *Alcedo atthis*

SIGN

NEST

Kingfishers are protected by law in the UK and it is an offence to disturb this species at or near the nest. Special licence must be sought to observe or photograph kingfishers at a nest site.

Kingfishers dig nest burrows in steep banks, usually bordering a waterway, but on occasion set a little way back from water. The key feature of a nest bank is its vertical or forward-leaning nature, preventing access to predators such as stoat, weasel and mink. Holes tend to be a metre or more above the water, and 50cm down from the top edge. They are dug singly, and are circular or slightly oval in shape, being marginally higher than they are wide. Tunnel length varies from about 50cm to well over a metre, with an ovoid chamber excavated at the end.

Active nests may be identified by fresh digging activity early in the season, leading to a clean-looking entrance hole during incubation. Once chicks hatch, the nest tunnel

SIZE

Weight: 40g
Length: 16cm
Wingspan: 25cm

KINGFISHER'S YEAR

Egg laying: 1 or 2 broods, occasionally 3 from early April

Clutch size: 6–7 eggs

Incubation: 23–27 days

Fledging: 24–25 days

Young are driven out of the parents' territory just a few days after fledging, in preparation for the next brood

Despite their strikingly colourful plumage, kingfishers blend in remarkably well with bankside vegetation, especially if they are exposing the orange chest rather than the blue feathers on the back.

[TOP] Where kingfishers regularly perch and fish, their projectile droppings streak the nearby branches and vegetation. Unlike many bird droppings, they are startlingly white, with no black content.

[ABOVE] Most kingfisher pellets are cast directly into the water and so are never found. Occasionally, though, you may discover one on a rock or jetty below a favoured perch. They contain small fish bones and scales, aquatic insect remains and amphibian bones.

becomes increasingly soiled as they defecate, aiming their faeces towards the light of the entrance. Towards the end of the nestling stage, black slimy deposit may run from the lower lip of the entrance hole and down the bank a short way. One sniff of an active nest immediately informs the observer of its smelly contents!

Occasionally kingfishers choose to dig tunnels in the muddy root balls of fallen trees or to adopt existing tunnels such as drainage culverts. They sometimes use artificial nest tunnels and chambers where offered.

A kingfisher flying with a fish in its beak (facing head out) is preparing to deliver the meal either to a mate – early on in the season the male offers many treats to his mate – or to a chick. Nest locations may be narrowed down by careful observation of bird's flying behaviour and the repetitious nature of routes to and from a nest.

Most nests do not have obvious perches immediately outside the tunnel entrance, but nearby perches may have telltale droppings below them.

OTHER SIGN

Unusually among birds, droppings can inform the observer of the presence of kingfishers. You may, for instance, spot their projectile excretions on vegetation beneath perches that allow the bird to study the water. These have a brilliant white appearance, often leaving linear streaks 2–5cm in length and rarely if ever showing any solid black elements.

Kingfishers cast pellets of undigested prey remains. These are almost exclusively fish bones and scales, though aquatic insect remains may also be present. The vast majority of these fall into water, but every now and then they can be found on man-made structures such as jetties or on banks free of vegetation. They are small, often teardrop shaped and usually grey or grey-black in colour.

Kingfishers announce their whereabouts with regular calls as they fly to and fro, especially on linear waterways like narrow streams and rivers. The piercing, high-pitched mono- or disyllabic call is the observer's best clue to the imminent approach of the bird – which is just as well, since kingfishers fly low and fast. Without this early warning, they will flash past unnoticed.

HOW TO WATCH

Once you know what a kingfisher call sounds like, you will start to see the birds much more frequently. As mentioned previously, they announce their imminent arrival around a bend in a river or across open water with their high-pitched piercing whistles. With a few exceptions, such as in areas of very high benign human traffic (canals, public parks and so on) kingfishers are shy of humans. This is a legacy of having been heavily persecuted for their plumage in the past, both to adorn ladies' hats and for fishing flies. Thankfully, both uses have been illegal for decades, but the British kingfisher tribe has an inherited and quite reasonable distrust of people.

Kingfishers, however, respond with indifference to new inanimate objects alongside or even within a waterway, and so can be watched and photographed from portable hides, or using simple but comprehensive camouflage. Where kingfishers regularly hunt, a hide will be accepted, even in quite close proximity. If you have a licence from the relevant authority, photography or observation at the nest site can also be conducted using a hide and only a short introductory period of a day or so for the structure is necessary (see page 24 for more about portable hide use).

I have successfully used screens made from dense clumps of reeds and grasses to watch and film kingfishers. And my friend and colleague, Sam Stewart, has used a ghillie suit to take 'selfies' with kingfishers sitting on his head!

If there are no suitable perches along a waterway, kingfishers readily take to an introduced perch. They favour a perch that lies horizontally parallel to the water's surface, so choose a branch which curls up, then over to achieve this before setting it into the soil on the river or lake bank. Once you have introduced a suitable perch, leave it in position for a week or more before considering staking it out with a hide.

Most photographs of kingfishers diving for fish involve a tank or corral into which live fish have been introduced. Wild kingfishers readily visit a regular and reliable food source and it is with this in mind that feeding stations containing live fish are created to provide views and opportunities for images both above and below the water's surface. If this tactic is to be used, the welfare of the fish in any holding environment must be carefully considered.

In the past, I have filmed and photographed kingfishers inside their nest chamber (under a schedule 1 licence). This was very intrusive and took many weeks to achieve without disturbing the parent birds. I would now advocate only trying to attract a kingfisher pair into a purpose-built artificial nest tunnel and chamber with a view to taking images of them as they raise a family.

OTHER BIRDS

HERON
Ardea cinerea

This large bird is widespread and relatively easy to see over most of the UK. Protracted close views depend either on the observer not being detected or the heron population being sufficiently tolerant of human presence.

In areas where herons are nervous, a hide is necessary for good views. I have had wonderfully intimate encounters using portable hides, and good results working from a vehicle with scrim across the viewing window. In places where herons are used to high levels of benign human activity, such as in urban parks and along canals, they ignore the observer and can even be encouraged to feed on fresh raw whole fish.

GANNET
Morus bassanus

At their nesting colonies, gannets can be fantastically confiding, even aggressive towards an observer. Many colonies are on steep cliffs, making access impossible without technical climbing gear and experience, but some colonies have spilled on to flatter areas on the tops of cliffs, and here you can approach to within a metre or so of nests.

When hunting gannets zero in on a shoal of fish, they go into a rapid frenzy of feeding, plunge-diving and calling excitedly. If you are in boat, it is possible to get among the birds with little disruption of their feeding behaviour. Due to a legacy of following fishing boats, many gannets will also come readily to fresh fish being proffered. Once the first bird has caught on to the free meal, many others are likely to follow, and with sufficient fish available you may soon be surrounded by hundreds of these huge seabirds, plunge-diving within a few metres of the side of the boat.

PASSERINES

This large group of perching birds includes species such as the blackbird and nightingale, as well as the tit family, robin and many others.

Many passerines respond well to song or call mimicry, none more so than the cuckoo, the male of which comes readily to investigate a well-mimicked cuckoo call. I use the falsetto range of my voice for this.

More generally, the trick of 'pishing' is well known among bird watchers, especially in North America, where generic mimicry of small perching bird alarm and mobbing calls brings other small birds close, as they attempt to catch sight of the danger. As the name suggests, a 'psshhhh' sound is produced by expelling air through clenched teeth, which sounds a little like the alarm call of a small bird.

Feeding stations are a great way to attract and get close views of small birds, and the wider the variety of foods and feeders you offer, the more species you are likely to attract.

HIRUNDINES

Swallows and house martins both build cup- or dome-shaped nests out of small blobs of mud. To encourage either species to visit a viewing area, create a pool with muddy margins, or simply an area of wet soil, preferably one that is not too sandy. Do this in early spring, to coincide with the arrival of these summer migrants to European shores, when they are keen to build new nests or reinforce last year's structures. Once you know your mud pool is being visited by hirundines, observe from a portable hide.

Sand martins dig their nest holes in vertically faced sand banks and so do not respond to this method.

WILDFOWL

A broad group of birds that includes all swan, duck and goose species.

Most freshwater ducks can be observed with ease in their wetland habitats, and many have adapted to life alongside humans and will readily come to proffered food.

Coastal duck species, such as scoter, can be more tricky to watch since they feed on open water and tend to be nervous of humans. The exception is the eider duck, which is common around northern coastlines with some populations being tolerant of humans and allowing close observation. It is also possible to attract courting eider ducks by mimicking the drake's 'oooooh' call. This sounds very like a person responding to a juicy bit of gossip and can be reproduced with the human voice.

Many wild geese, such as barnacle, brent, white-fronted and pink-footed are notoriously flighty, and with good reason. For thousands of years they have been a prized by humans as a source of meat and to this day they are targeted. Close observation of wild goose flocks requires the careful introduction of a portable hide in favoured feeding grounds or the use of established public hides on nature reserves.

Well-used feeding sites will be littered with droppings. Depending on the species, these vary in size, but all are compact and cylindrical and comprise grasses and other vegetation. Even when geese have left their wintering grounds their droppings persist for many months.

Feral geese, such as the Canada goose and greylag, are easy to observe.

[CLOCKWISE FROM TOP LEFT] Swallow, gannet, goldeneye (drake), grey heron, mandarin (drake), mute swan, Shetland wren, bullfinch male [CENTRE].

ADDER *Vipera berus*

Length: 50–80cm (including tail)
Larger in northern Europe

This is the only venomous snake in the UK and so should be given due respect. That said, adders are not aggressive and they slip away into cover at the first hint of danger rather than use their bite as a defence. The effect of their venom on humans, though painful, is rarely fatal.

Adders leave no discoverable sign besides their shed skin from time to time.

SEASON

Adders emerge from hibernation in the early spring, and by April are ready to mate. Observation in this period can be very rewarding, since males are ranging over territories in search of receptive females and several males may congregate on the same spot, actively vying for the right to mate.

A male searching for a receptive female moves with a particular action, twitching forwards in short bursts and regularly testing the air with his tongue. Once the male reaches the female he approaches her with very deliberate twitching movements, and when he is close enough to touch her will tap his chin against her back and sides. If another male arrives on the scene, a fight may ensue. Both males rise up, chest to chest, each trying to wrestle the other to the ground. They do not attempt to bite each other.

Eggs are held within the body of the female until they are ready to hatch, when the 'live' young are born. This usually occurs around midsummer.

HOW TO WATCH

Adders are widespread but uncommon over most of Britain, frequenting heaths, moors, woodland edge and raised areas of wetland. Choose a sunny morning in spring (from early April over most of the UK) for the best chance of spotting one.

Walk slowly, with soft footfalls, and be aware of how your outline is silhouetted against the sky, as well as where your shadow is likely to fall. Try to avoid it falling on the areas you think are likely to host adders.

From a distance, study places that may be suitable basking spots – sunny patches at the bottom of bramble, gorse, bracken or close to the base of drystone walls.

Use your binoculars to study in detail anything that catches your eye. Develop your search image (page 20) – adders blend beautifully into their environment and the zigzag pattern down their back looks very like the shadow cast by bracken leaves.

Once you have spotted the coiled form of a basking snake, watch it from a distance. Adders will tolerate an observer as close as two or three metres if your approach is slow and gentle, but any movement will catch their eye and disturb them, and the vibrations from a heavy footfall will also send them off into cover.

If you do disturb an adder that has already sensed your presence and headed off into the vegetation, find a spot which

gives you a clear view of where it was resting and settle there. In time, the adder is likely to return to its basking site.

This species displays great site fidelity if undisturbed, and female adders especially may bask by day in the same spot, and rest in the same cover. Outside the breeding season, it is often possible to find one or more snakes using the same or similar sunning patches throughout much of the summer when conditions allow. Adders, other snakes and slow worms,

will use refugia – a sheet of material such as corrugated iron, carpet tiles or Onduline roofing that warms up in the morning sun. By placing these on the ground around suitable habitat, and carefully lifting them from time to time, it may be possible to see the reptiles beneath.

The adder is beautifully camouflaged in its environment, especially among gorse and bracken. The leaf forms mirror the zigzag pattern on the snake's back.

GRASS SNAKE *Natrix natrix*

SIZE
Length: females are up to 1.9m, though 1m is more usual; males are smaller and rarely longer than 50cm

SEASON
Grass snake hibernation usually lasts from October to April. This is an active species that ranges widely in search of its prey, which is made up largely of amphibians – frogs, toads and newts. It will also take fish.

Mating occurs in the spring, when several males vie to mate with the larger female, twisting and writhing over her body, though not fighting as such (see Adder page 232). Ten or more eggs are laid in June or July in piles of rotting vegetation, such as compost heaps – the high temperature of the heap helps with the incubation of the eggs. The eggs hatch six to eight weeks later.

SIGN
The rubbery shells of hatched eggs are quite commonly found in garden compost heaps. They are about 1.5cm long, whitish and oval shaped. The hole made by the emerging baby snake is obvious.

As the snakes grow, they shed their skin. Cast skins from every stage of the snake's development may be found caught in vegetation, usually close to the ground and often by bodies of still water – the grass snake's favoured habitat.

This is Britain's largest terrestrial reptile. Grass snakes are fast and sensitive to disturbance, often disappearing into cover long before you see them.

HOW TO WATCH

Though grass snakes bask, like most reptiles, they are wide ranging and do not show strong site fidelity. A careful study of open patches of ground near still water may be fruitful, though this species is observant and nervous and slips away at the slightest hint of danger. Mating balls of snakes may be less wary than usual, and you may be able to approach them more closely than you would a lone snake.

Like other snakes, grass snakes will readily use refugia that have been laid around suitable habitat, and careful observation of resting animals is possible by this method.

Observation of hunting snakes is difficult to plan and more likely to occur by chance. This species swims well and readily, and it may be possible to watch grass snakes hunting along the edges of still water bodies.

[TOP LEFT] The shed skin of a grass snake may be found tangled in vegetation.

SLOW WORM
Anguis fragilis

SMOOTH SNAKE
Coronella austriaca

Though unrelated (the slow worm is a legless lizard not a snake) both of these species are reclusive and rarely visible in the wild unless you turn over refugia to expose them. Smooth snakes (which are fully protected by law) may bask in the sun, but almost invariably do so in a tangle of thick vegetation, making them hard to see.

Slow worms may be seen away from cover at dusk and dawn, but tend to spend most of their time beneath logs or other cover, foraging for slugs and small bugs by rooting around in dense vegetation, compost heaps and the like.

[TOP RIGHT] Slow worms look like snakes, but are in fact legless lizards.

SAND LIZARD *Lacerta agilis*

SEASON

This species is fully protected by law. Like all reptiles in the region, sand lizards hibernate, emerging in the early spring (late March or April), then courting and mating soon after.

Eggs are laid in May or early June and hatch in late August or September.

SIZE
Length: up to 20cm

SIGN

This species is very closely associated with its preferred habitat of sandy heathland and dunes. Nesting banks of firm sand that face the warming sun for a good part of the day are chosen by the females, who then dig burrows where they lay their eggs. The entrances to these burrows have distinctive, half dome shaped-roofs, with flatter bases, and measure about 2–3cm across and 1–2cm high.

Both female [BELOW LEFT] and male [BELOW RIGHT] sand lizards emerge from hibernation in spring and may be spotted basking on vegetation on the ground. They keep close to cover and disappear at the first sign of danger.

Common lizards, like other reptiles, are much more likely to be seen on warm sunny days, especially in spring when they emerge from hibernation.

HOW TO WATCH

Passive observation of sand lizards is possible in suitable habitat. During the mating season, the brightly coloured males vie for the attention of females and may fight, wrestling and biting each other. These battles cause significant noise in the vegetation, often at the base of bracken or gorse bushes, and may draw the attention of the observer. Once a known sunning spot has been established, careful observation may be made, though this species has good mid-distance eyesight and will run for cover if it spots any sudden movement.

Females preparing egg burrows may be seen digging in exposed sandy banks during May and early June. Passive 'sit-and-wait' observation is often fruitful, though great care should be taken not to move suddenly if the lizards are watching you. In some circumstances, a portable hide (page 24) may allow more relaxed and protracted views.

SIZE
Length: 10–15cm

COMMON LIZARD *Zootoca vivipara*

This species is widespread, can be found in most habitats, and is relatively easy to watch. It is easier to observe in the early morning when first warming up.

Like most reptiles, common lizards are sensitive to heavy vibrations and fast movements. Move slowly and deliberately, paying special attention to your footfall and hand and arm movements, keeping all to a minimum. The first sign you may get of a lizard nearby is the sound of one scuttling in the vegetation. Even though this almost certainly means you have disturbed it, it is worth freezing on the spot and carefully scouring the surrounding vegetation for the source of the sound.

Once you have spotted a lizard you can approach very slowly to within about two metres or less without sending it off into cover. This species will respond to the introduction of an artificial fly (see Raft spider page 250).

COMMON FROG *Rana temporaria*

SEASON

Frogs hibernate in the northern winter, typically from late October to January. Some male frogs may lie dormant in the mud at the bottom of ponds at this time, but most frogs find suitable hibernacula in log and rock piles or other damp sites that remain a constant temperature through the colder months.

This species is usually the first amphibian to emerge in the spring, and in some parts of southern England spawn may be seen in late January if conditions allow. In most areas, breeding takes place in March/April. Males are often the first to reach the breeding areas (usually still water with shallow margins and aquatic vegetation) and begin calling.

Females arriving at the breeding pond are grappled by the males, one of which will successfully grip his mate around the waist using his forelegs in an embrace known as amplexus. Competing males are rejected by the victor with forceful kicks from his hind legs, though 'frog balls' sometimes occur when several males grip a single female from different angles.

Spawn hatches 10–35 days after being laid (depending on temperature) and the tadpoles first feed on the jelly mass of the egg before moving off to graze on algae in the pond. Vast shoals of tadpoles my be seen swimming in rings or figures of eight on warm spring days. They are almost certainly feeding on algal blooms, though this shoaling behaviour is still not fully understood. As the tadpoles mature, they move from a vegetarian to a carnivorous diet, before emerging in early summer as fully formed froglets. Baby frogs venture out of their natal pond on a warm, damp day, and thousands may litter the ground as they radiate out and away from the water.

SIGN

Frogs leave little or no sign. The most likely clue that this species frequents an area will be their spawn, tadpoles or the remains of adults that have been killed by predators. Frogs are eaten by virtually everything that takes live prey from time to time, from herons, grass snakes, mink and otters to badgers,

SIZE
Female slightly larger than male
Length: 6–9 cm from nose to vent

In late spring, frog tadpoles may shoal en masse, forming wriggling black slicks in ponds and lake margins.

rats, foxes and a variety of birds. Gravid females, caught by otters, are brought ashore to be eaten and clumps of unlaid spawn (which is apparently distasteful to the feeding otter) mixed with some viscera are sometimes found on pond margins.

HOW TO WATCH

Outside the breeding season, frogs range far and wide, using any area of vegetation to seek out their invertebrate prey. The best time to observe frogs is when they congregate in their traditional breeding ponds. The trigger for this activity is closely linked to temperature and the start varies significantly from year to year. Breeding activity may take place over a few days or weeks depending on conditions. The first warm, damp night of the year is often a cue to go out and check breeding ponds for activity.

Once night has fallen, approach the pond carefully and quietly. Do not shine white torchlight on the water and, once you have reached a point within a few metres of the margin, switch off all artificial light and listen. Male frogs call to draw the females to the breeding arena, and their low soft croaking is a sure sign of activity. Having established the rough position of the congregating males, you can use a torch to get a view of those frogs which are at or near the surface. A red filter across the torch is less likely to cause disturbance, and will allow more protracted views. If the breeding activity is in full swing, frogs will continue throughout daylight hours, though rarely with the same numbers and vigour as they display after dark.

Once all the breeding females have deposited their spawn, the frogs disperse, some finding nooks and crannies around the pond margin to rest during the day before venturing forth to look for invertebrates by night. Most leave the pond to forage in the surrounding habitats.

[ABOVE] Spawn is laid in early spring, often when frosts are still likely. Soon after breeding, adult frogs disperse, emerging on land at night to feed on invertebrates.

COMMON TOAD *Bufo bufo*

SEASON

Toads usually emerge later in the spring than frogs and make the journey to the breeding pond overland during the hours of darkness. 'Toad nights' are warm and wet, though there is not usually heavy rain, and often begin in March in Britain.

Males are usually the first to emerge from hibernation, but it is not unusual to find pairs in amplexus making their way to the breeding pond, with the male getting a free lift on the female's back!

Males may stay in the pond for several weeks, but the females leave the water soon after spawning.

Long, double strings of spawn are laid and wrapped around aquatic vegetation as the pair meander through the water from March onwards. It usually takes about three weeks to hatch into shoals of tadpoles, with the toadlets finally emerging in June or July.

SIZE
Length: F 8–15cm; M 7–9cm

SIGN

Toads leave little or no visible sign. While they do shed their skin from time to time, this is usually eaten by the toad itself, though fragments of jelly-like shed skin may be found clinging to aquatic vegetation. Once out of the breeding pond, they use a regular retreat during daylight hours such as under a log pile or a pile of stones, and a patch of slightly worn vegetation at the entrance to the lair may betray their foot traffic.

At breeding ponds, dead toads may be found around the margin or on the water's edge. A close look will usually reveal injuries sustained from the teeth of mammalian predators such as otters and foxes which, having bitten the toad, get a mouthful of the noxious bufotoxin produced by the amphibian's paratoid glands – the swollen areas behind the eyes. While these dead toads have paid the price of being an experimental meal, animals that have tried eating a toad like this rarely attempt to do so again. There are predators, such as grass snakes, that are unaffected by the bufotoxin.

Toad spawn is laid in strings, as opposed to the clumps of spawn laid by frogs.

Strings of spawn with parallel ribbons of eggs can be seen in early spring, stretched around aquatic vegetation.

HOW TO WATCH

Like frogs, toads are best observed when breeding. They are at their most active after dark on warm, damp nights, with the highest levels of activity from about an hour after dark to before midnight.

Where migrating toads have to cross roads, hundreds may be seen on a single night and thousands are killed. They are sensitive to artificial light, but tolerate a dim torch or one fitted with a red filter. Once in the pond, males call, emitting their high, ringing single note croak to attract mates. They also use a similar sounding 'release' call when another male attempts to grip them in amplexus or tries to muscle in on the female they have already paired with. These sounds carry a fair distance and are a good sign that there are toads in a body of water.

[ABOVE] Toads are often seen on land, usually at night but also during the day in early spring and the breeding season.

NEWTS

SEASON

All newts in the UK spend the majority of their lives away from water, either hibernating through the winter months or foraging for their invertebrate prey through the hours of darkness. By day they retreat to damp hideaways under logs or stones. They come to water only to breed, usually arriving in a pond or other body of still water in late February or March and staying until June.

SIGN

A careful examination of any small-leafed pond weed in the spring may reveal newt eggs, each wrapped carefully in a leaf. They may be laid singly, or in small, loose clusters of three or four, depending on the size of the leaf.

HOW TO WATCH

A careful vigil of suitable habitat will eventually reveal the presence of newts as they surface to take a gulp of air, before sinking back into the weed or bottom of the pond. Checking under refugia, such as logs, in the vicinity of a pond may reveal newts that have left the water or have yet to make their way there. Using a powerful torch to scan the pond margins at night may also reveal the animals, which are much more active during the hours of darkness.

Once you have established that newts are present, a mask and snorkel can provide excellent views of breeding behaviour. Watch out for females egg laying, using their hind feet to wrap a leaf of aquatic weed around each egg as it is laid.

Courtship involves a male positioning himself in front of a female and fanning water along his flank and into her face. If she is receptive, the passing of the spermatophore is done remotely – the pair walking in procession, the male depositing spermatophore from his gonads on the bed of the pond, and the female moving over it and collecting it in her cloaca. All newts are protected by law and you need a licence to handle great crested newts.

GREAT CRESTED NEWT
Triturus cristatus

Length: up to 15cm
Largest of the UK newts

SMOOTH NEWT
Lissotriton vulgaris

Length: up to 10cm
Spotted throat

PALMATE NEWT
Lissotriton helveticus

Length: up to 9cm
No spots on throat

[OPPOSITE TOP] Smooth newt male in breeding colours.
[OPPOSITE CENTRE] Smooth newt female.
[OPPOSITE BOTTOM] Palmate newt male in breeding colours.

BUTTERFLIES

There are currently 59 species of butterfly breeding in the UK and a few others that appear as migrants. Every species of butterfly has a specific life cycle and flight period that dictates when it is best to see it in the field. Some species are adult and on the wing for only a very brief period in the year; others are around for longer or may have multiple adult emergences depending on their breeding cycle or migration. There are excellent books and online resources available that outline in detail the European species and give specific details of when each is likely to be on the wing.

HOW TO WATCH

Observation techniques for butterflies differ according to the species you are trying to watch, as they vary hugely in their reaction to the approach of a human observer. The familiar small tortoiseshell, for example, can be very accommodating, while some of the fritillaries can be super flighty! Life habits also influence the opportunities you may have of spotting a certain species. Many butterflies keep to open country and low-level shrubs and flowers and so are within easy reach of an observer. Others spend a lot of time in the high canopy of mature trees and it can be really challenging to spot or get close views of them.

For the closest, most protracted views, start your butterfly watching early in the morning or on an overcast day; cooler air renders them more sluggish than they are on a hot day.

A warm sunny day encourages more butterflies to be on the wing, making them easier to spot in the first place, but conversely more likely to fly away at the first hint of danger.

If you spot a butterfly on the wing, keep your eye on it and focus on the point where it appears to alight. Approach this point slowly, bearing in mind your silhouette against the sky from the butterfly's point of view, and keep hand and arm movements to a minimum. Be careful to note where your shadow falls as you get close to your subject, being careful not to allow it to fall across the butterfly you are trying to watch.

Good-quality, close-focusing binoculars (page 6) are a huge asset when spotting and identifying butterfly species in the field. They are especially useful for watching the smaller varieties such as the blues and skippers, which may blend well with the vegetation once they have settled and display very subtle differences between species.

The 'sit-and-wait' method at a suitable patch of flowers can be very rewarding and may offer the most intimate and protracted views. Simply identify a nectar-bearing flower in a good location on a sunny summer's day and settle within a couple of metres of it for close views of the visitors as they pop in to feed.

You can also attract butterflies to a feeder as follows.

BUTTERFLY FEEDING STATION
100g unrefined granulated sugar
900ml water
Overripe fruit, such as bananas or pears

For the sugar solution, boil the water in a small saucepan. Add the sugar and simmer gently until it is fully dissolved, then allow it to cool completely. Any solution not used immediately can be stored in the fridge for up to a week. For the fruit, simply collect any overripe fruit and set it aside with the moist flesh exposed.

You will need:
a brightly coloured plastic plate (red, yellow, blue or purple are good colours)
string
any shallow plastic pot with a lip (small yoghurt pots are ideal)
a brightly coloured nylon dish scourer

Butterflies are attracted to bright colours and reflected UV light which they see in the flowers they normally target for nectar. Bear this in mind when making your butterfly feeder.

Some butterfly species, including red admirals, overwinter as adults so feed well in autumn in order to survive their hibernation.

▶ Cut a hole in the centre of the plastic plate to allow the shallow plastic pot to slide in, while ensuring that the lip on the pot prevents it sliding through completely.
▶ Pierce the plastic plate at four evenly spaced points around its rim. Thread four pieces of string, each about 40cm long, through these holes and tie knots on the underside to create a hanging platform.
▶ Hang your butterfly feeding platform from a low branch or other horizontal fixing in a sunny spot, sheltered from the wind, in the garden.
▶ Stuff the nylon scourer into the yoghurt pot so that it is level with or just below the top of the pot (you may have to cut the pad if it doesn't fit easily).
▶ Pour enough of the sugar solution into the pot to bring it a millimetre or so below the top surface of the scourer.
▶ Slot the pot with its pad and sugar solution into the central hole in the plate.
▶ Place small pieces of rotting fruit around the periphery of the plate. Clean the entire surface weekly.

DRAGONFLIES AND DAMSELFLIES

With almost 60 species of dragonfly and damselfly in the UK, this is a group of insects that is as varied as it is beautiful.

There are excellent identification guides available to help you learn more about these most visually striking insects, but for the purposes of this book I shall deal with them as two distinct types.

The distinction between damselflies (suborder Zygoptera) and dragonflies (suborder Anisoptera) can be broadly described as follows.

▶ Dragonflies at rest hold their paired wings out at their sides, looking like a fixed-wing aircraft.
▶ The eyes of a dragonfly meet over the top of the head.
▶ Damselflies at rest fold their wings more or less along their backs.
▶ The eyes of a damselfly are separated by its face and head.

Damsels (as they are sometimes described) are mostly delicate creatures of open standing water. Two species (the demoiselles) are more closely associated with running water. Dragonflies tend to stick to open standing water or the surrounding countryside.

HOW TO WATCH

Each species of dragonfly or damselfly in the UK has a flight period, when the adult flying imagos emerge from their aquatic nymph state. In most years, any time from late May through to mid-September is good, with June to August being the busiest period for most species. None of these insects enjoys cold weather, so to stand the best chance of good sightings, choose a hot and sunny day. Just sitting patiently by any suitable body of fresh water on a good day should bring you super views of a number of different species. For close views, and especially for photographing these creatures, certain techniques can be helpful.

Some groups, such as the chasers and skimmers (*Libellula* sp., *Orthetrum* sp.), repeatedly return to the same perch. This is especially true of territorial males. Once you have established a favoured resting point, carefully move close by and wait for the insect to return. If there is a shortage of suitable perches, introducing a stick will almost certainly result in it being adopted by a chaser or skimmer within half an hour or so. This applies even if you hold the stick in your hands, like a fishing rod.

Keep all movement to an absolute minimum; most dragonflies and damselflies have excellent eyesight and will move away if they feel in the least bit threatened.

The larger hawkers (*Aeshna* sp.), are dynamic flyers and rarely come to rest on prominent perches, choosing instead dense vegetation when they do settle. Male emperors (*Anax imperator*) and other hawkers (*Aeshna* sp.) spend hours quartering back and forth across a body of water, snatching small flying insects to eat and chasing other males out of their territory. Females are pursued by the males and they couple. This coupling may draw your attention due to the noisy clattering

of wings as the pair wrestle in tandem. Once mating has occurred, the female separates from the male and finds suitable emergent water vegetation on which to lay her eggs. This she does by alighting on the vegetation and thrusting her abdomen beneath the water surface, sometimes half submerging her entire body in the process.

With care and patience, egg-laying, or ovipositing, females may be very closely observed. Here again, keep movement to a minimum and, if you must move a hand or other part of your body, do so in a very slow and considered fashion. Dragonflies and damselflies will give no warning that they are disturbed until the moment they take off and fly away.

Other species remain in tandem even once mated. This is true of the darters (*Sympetrum* sp.) and many of the damselflies.

Males grip the females around the neck, back of head or prothorax, depending on the species, using their anal appendages, or claspers. Damselfly species tend to land on emergent vegetation and the couple

move down until the female can lay eggs beneath the water's surface. Some species completely submerge while egg laying. Others, such as the darter species, dip repeatedly down to the water, lightly touching the surface with the female's abdomen and scattering eggs.

On a warm early summer's morning keep a careful eye out for emergent dragonflies and damselflies. Scour the base of vegetation, like bulrushes, for nymphs climbing clear of the water and ascending the stem. Even then, the nymph is sensitive to movement and may abandon its emergence attempt if disturbed. Wait for the nymph to settle completely before attempting to get a very close view of the dragon or damselfly nymph splitting down the back and the adult flying imago emerging from its old skin.

Dragonfly species use a variety of techniques to find their prey. Hawkers (such as this southern hawker, *Aeshna cyanea*) patrol their territory on the wing, dipping to snatch flies from the air.

MOTHS

More than 2,400 species of moth have been recorded in the UK and, like butterflies, each has a flight period depending on species. Late summer and early autumn are great times to moth watch.

Some species are positively phototactic – that is to say, attracted to light – and can be collected for observation with a moth trap. This is a device that uses a bright light attached to a box with a funnel in the centre. Set it up in the evening and leave it to run through the night,. Moths that are attracted to the light will drop into the box via the funnel and can be viewed at your leisure the following morning.

A simpler method of observation which exploits phototactic species is to shine a light on to a white sheet hanging from a line. Peg or weigh the bottom of the sheet to the ground to prevent it flapping unduly. Moths and other insects will alight on the sheet after dark and can be observed before they fly off.

Some moth species are not drawn to light but may be attracted to nectar. These can be brought close to the observer with the use of wine ropes. Here is the recipe.

WINE ROPE

1 x 70cl bottle of inexpensive red wine
1kg unrefined granulated sugar
500g dark treacle
2 dessertspoons of honey
small glass of dark rum

Put the wine into a large saucepan and warm it gently over a medium heat. Add the sugar, treacle and honey and stir. Don't add the rum just yet.

Allow the mixture to cool, stirring in any crystallising sugars that may form on the top as it cools.

Decant the mix into a medium to large bucket that has a sealable top – plastic paint kettles from DIY stores are ideal.

You will need:

3–4 metres of absorbent cord or rope
(window sash cord is ideal), cut into
4 lengths of about 1 metre each
4 clothes pegs
rubber gloves
a torch

▸ Put all the rope into the bucket of sugared wine solution at least an hour before dusk.
▸ Just before use, add the rum to the mix and stir.
▸ Choose a warm, humid evening and night. Take your bucket of soaked rope and all the other equipment into the garden or area you wish to bait. With gloved hands, take out each rope in turn, give it a gentle shake, and hang it with a clothes peg from a low branch or fence, or drape it over vegetation such as bramble bushes.
▸ Retire until darkness falls, then check your ropes with a torch from time to time during the first few hours of darkness. While many moth species are attracted to light, there are some that are not and among these are species such as the Old Lady Moth, which will home in on your boozy sugared ropes for a sip,
▸ Once you have finished your night's observations, put your ropes back in the solution for another night. The solution lasts for a week or so if kept cool.

GRASSHOPPERS

These insects are not normally considered within the scope of a fieldcraft book, but it is possible to improve your views of some species with a bit of mimicry, hence their inclusion here.

MARSH GRASSHOPPER

This is one of the largest grasshoppers in the region, with one of the least impressive 'songs'. The gentle ticking made by a stridulating male is a sound heard in some southern wet heaths.

You can entice both male and female closer to you by mimicking a stridulating male. Lie on your belly in suitable habitat and produce a tutting sound with your tongue against the roof of your mouth. Be careful to replicate the rhythm of the grasshoppers around you; generally about one 'tick' per second.

MEADOW GRASSHOPPER

This common grasshopper is the sound of late summer in grasslands. Once you have identified a stridulating male, mimic his song by drawing a credit card rapidly across a fine-toothed comb. With practice, you will make a fair approximation of the sound and should get a response from males and females alike, which will trundle through the grass towards you.

SPIDERS

There are more than 650 species of spider in the UK, occupying a wide variety of habitats from caves to sand dunes, as well as human habitation. Many of them mature in late summer and early autumn, making this the ideal time to go spider watching.

Most spiders are confiding and, if visible, tolerate the observer at close quarters. A handful of species that have acute mid-distance eyesight, such as raft spiders, may react adversely to movement, and most species will retreat if they feel heavy vibrations.

RAFT SPIDERS
Dolomedes sp.

The largest spiders in the UK, raft spiders live in wetland habitats, particularly pools in southern heath and moorland. This spider uses the water's surface as its web, feeling for vibrations across the surface meniscus through its feet. It usually dashes up to 10cm across the surface of the pond to grab prey stuck in the surface, but can also break through the surface tension and reach down into the water to grab prey. This may be anything from a tadpole to a small fish, or even another raft spider.

You can get great views of raft spiders by slowly walking around ponds, scouring the bankside vegetation at or near the water's surface. You may spot their robust figures, reaching out from a tangle of reeds or even resting in full view.

You can also elicit hunting behaviour by using a small fishing fly. Cut the hook from the fly with wire cutters, attach it to fine monofilament fishing line and then to a stick which will act as your 'spidering' rod. Once you have spotted a spider, very slowly introduce your lure on the water's surface, then drag it closer to the spider. If all goes well, the spider will feel the vibrations on the surface, see the fake fly, then dash out and grapple it, sinking its venomous fangs in to make its 'kill'. Most spiders let go soon after they realise they have been duped, but I have had some

that were more tenacious and clung on to the lure so tightly that I could gently lift their forequarters off the water.

ORB WEB SPIDERS
includes *Araneus* sp.

These include the common garden cross spiders and many others.

Orb webs show up well on a misty morning in late summer and early autumn. When the spiders are mature, their webs are at their biggest and the threads are most visible when coated with beads of dew. Even on days when there is no mist, you can get better views of webs by introducing a mist of your own. With an ordinary handheld atomiser (the sort used to moisten the leaves of house plants), spray across a bush that appears to have webs in it. You may be surprised by just how many individual webs there are in the one place, as they are suddenly revealed in all their bejewelled, dewy glory. The maker of the web may be sitting in the centre of the orb (as is often the case with cross spiders) or in a retreat of leaves or other cover, keeping one leg on an indicator line that feels for vibrations in the web.

You can get spiders to come out and check their webs for prey by pretending to be a fly. Simply pick a fine stem of grass, allow one end of it to lightly touch the web near its centre and gently wobble the other end. This is a fairly blunt instrument, however, and if you are too heavy handed some spiders may not be fooled into thinking a fly has hit their web. Instead they may take evasive action, believing there to be a predator nearby.

A more refined method is to use a tuning fork that vibrates at around 426 Hz, producing the note 'A'. This approximates the vibrations of a trapped fly trying to escape and is likely to bring the web's owner out to attack. Simply strike the fork to set it vibrating, then gently touch one arm against the web.

This method works for orb web species but is equally effective on webs where the spider retreats into a tunnel. These include house spiders (*Tegenaria* sp.) and tube web spiders (*Segestria* sp.).

On calm days in autumn and spring, you may witness masses of spiders 'ballooning'. This occurs when the young of some spiders, and also smaller species like Linyphiidae, undertake migrations by 'flying' on the breeze. Watch for small spiders climbing fence posts, or tall vegetation. Once at the summit they turn to face the wind, allow fine strands of silk to exude from their spinnerets and, when the moment is right, release their grip from their perch to be taken on the breeze to pastures new. On some days entire fields are coated with the threads of silk, a phenomenon known as angel hair.

During a ballooning event, any high point will be adopted by spiders searching for a launch pad, so a stick placed in the ground in the middle of suitable habitat is quickly adopted, allowing close observation and photography.

[OPPOSITE LEFT] Raft spiders are large, robust hunters in southern heathland ponds. They are powerful enough to reach through the water's surface and grab small fish.

[OPPOSITE RIGHT] Most orb web spiders mature in the late summer and early autumn. At this time their webs are larger and so more visible.

Index

ACKNOWLEDGEMENTS

I should like to thank my publisher, Quadrille, for keeping the belief that this book would be completed – eventually – and having the conviction to stick with me for the journey. Thank you to designers Emma and Alex, of Smith & Gilmour, for their clarity of vision which put order and form into the contents of my scattergun brain. Profuse thanks too go to my editor, Jinny Johnson, whose eye for detail and simultaneous ability to watch things develop from a height, has kept everything on track with perspicacity, precision and good humour.

Over the years I have been allowed access to the most magical of nature reserves around the British Isles in my quest to photograph the wildlife there and I owe a debt of thanks to The Wildlife Trusts, the RSPB, the WWT, English Nature and the National Trust. Some of the images of mammals were taken in captivity, particularly the mustelids, and thanks go to Derek Gow for facilitating these. The ospreys were photographed at Horn Mill Trout Farm near Rutland Water. Huge thanks to the team there for allowing me access and keeping an eye out for the birds overhead!

Most of the images in the book are mine, but those that are not were taken by talented friends, who have allowed me to include their work to fill in the gaps. They are credited separately with page references to their work. Jake Davis has done a sterling job with the illustrations of each species and his speed, accuracy and willingness to tweak when I have been picky has been very much appreciated.

And finally thanks to all those who have put up with my obsessive focus on this project and who have facilitated its completion by supporting me when I have wobbled and for picking up the pieces I inevitably dropped along the way.

Simon King